ACKNOWLEDGEMENTS

I would like to thank Allison for being my great friend, confidant, editor, and critic.

But most of all for staying on my back about finishing this document.

She kept me in a positive frame of mind.

She gave me encouragement when I needed it the most.

Thank you, Allison

I would also like to thank my dear brother who has put up with me for 70 years.

Harassed me when we were children, just being a big brother.

For offering me constructive criticism when I needed to change course.

Thanks for giving me philosophical advice on my perspective of life in general.

For unknowingly starting me on my path to a greater understanding of life.

Thank you, Jon Mark.

Forword

Have you ever had something happen to you that you could not possibly explain? Have other people in your life had strange things happen to them and they tell you about it later? There are many things in our world that are unknown possibilities. Most people will not talk about extra normal experiences and just brush them aside--even though they cannot stop thinking about them. If you had an unusual feeling or event in your life, who can you talk to about it? Can you believe what you have been through or what you have heard? These experiences are more common than you would think and certainly not advertised. Our world is full of mystery and this unexplained weirdness exists all around us.

Mr. Stockton has had more exotic events and adventures than most people and met plenty of others who told him about even more odd unexplainable stories. In this book he describes dying twice and the many strange things that followed. He has had many psychic events and dreams and met regular folks who have been through the most bizarre happenings. What is real and what isn't? Who knows?

Unlock your fear of the unknown and listen to what cannot be explained. If you want a really different kind of true story, this is the book for you.

Allison S.

THE LUXURY of DISBELIEF

By Stephen A. Stockton

A Lifetime of Extraordinary Events

THE LUXURY OF DISBELIEF

Table of Contents

PREFACE--------------------page 11

INTRODUCTION--------------page 17

INTRODUCTION
PART ONE--page -------------page 34

PART ONE
Strange Memoirs
My Life in Years

FIVE
OBE------------------------------page 42

EIGHT
A Night Encounter-----------page 48

FIFTEEN
Second UFO Sighting---------page 58

SIXTEEN
Astral Travels-------------------page 63
OBE Experiences
Book of the Dead?
The Andromeda Trap
Bozo Nose
My Guardians and the Body Snatcher
Shadow Man?

SEVENTEEN
 A Shared Dream-------------page 97

EIGHTEEN
Impossible Beams of Light--page 103
A Terrifying Intrusion
The Philadelphia Experiment
 A Mothership
Grand Turino

TWENTY
It's that Simple--------------page 137
Pay Attention to Me

TWENTY-ONE
Hollow Men in the Dark--page 150

TWENTY-FIVE
Close Encounter w/Hairy--page 157

TWENTY-SIX
Two Iron Ships and a Girl-page 173
The Golden City
The Machine

TWENTY-EIGHT
A Séance and the Ouija
The Ouija Board------------page 202

THIRTY-ONE
Mexican Monolith--------page 208

THIRTY-SIX
Conspiracy Theories, Heaven's Gate, and the Atlantean Power Crystal---------------------- page 214

FORTY-TWO
A Light in the Hallway, Probes, and Night Terrors----------------------page 225

FORTY-FOUR
A Sad Reunion-----------page 235

FORTY-SIX
Stargate Confirmation--page 240

FORTY-SEVEN
Nasal Surgery and
a Revelation----------------page 245

FIFTY
The Elemental-------------page 249

FIFTY-FIVE
An Egyptian Merchant
Dream Vision---------------page 258

FIFTY-SIX
A Potato Chip, Remote Viewing,
And a Human Operating
System----------------------page 262

FIFTY-NINE
The Gift---------------------page 272

SIXTY
A China Syndrome------page 276

SIXTY-ONE
Gaia Vision--------------- page 280

SIXTY-TWO
Three Knocks-------------page 286

SIXTY-THREE
Falling Things--------page 287

SIXTY-FIVE
A Red Ring-----------page 292

SIXTY-SIX
Two Red Rings
and Claws------------page 294

SIXTY-NINE
A Shot in the
Dark-----------------page 298

CONCLUSION
PART ONE-----------page 305

Preface

When it comes to complicated or frightening truths there are two kinds of people. The first is the type that is willing to face the truth and then there are those who will bury their heads in the sand and pretend that all is right in the world. Sometimes it can be too much. I sympathize with you. But not to see both is folly. Much is right with the world but sadly there is much that is not. All that is not good is of human design. We all know we live in a dualistic reality. Almost all will choose one side or the other. But there is another choice, that is to embrace both equally. Personally, I want, and need to embrace both. Lessons can be learned from both. For those who embrace the hard truths I applaud your fearlessness. For those that do not, I understand. After all, the world can be a cruel place.

I do not admonish those who live in the luxury of disbelief. Life is often frightening and uncertain. I have been there myself. This document is a testament to those fears.

The world of nature is a beautiful creation, please do not forget that. It is the corruption of the collective of mankind that makes the world the hell hole it has become whether it is from laziness, fear, deception, or ignorance. Our civilization has risen to new heights of technology as well as the beauty we have created in art, music, poetry, etc. There is much beauty in the world. Each person has their own story to tell.

One cannot change a problem by thinking the same way that created the problem in the first place, one cannot change anything without changing the way one thinks. One must elevate the mind to elevate the world. We have many challenges to overcome. We may be pushed to the brink of extinction. We have once, maybe many times before, but I believe we will come through it better than before. We are a tenacious group. We now have help, unseen forces that are here to guide us. We find ourselves being awakened to the evil truths of the world but will no longer tolerate the evil that has infected this planet. Many are now asking the questions that very few have voiced before.

In the beginning of the Renaissance our race took a wrong turn. We switched from a predominately wholistic mindset to the predominately rational mindset which has given us many improvements but at what cost. There too many to name. We have lost our spiritual mindset but the scale was still not balanced between the two and it still is not to this day. Greed is our greatest enemy. We are awakening to the truth that we have been manipulated for a very long time and here we are now in the endgame.

Through the following events of my life, my mind has been elevated enough, seasoned enough to understand this. Like many, I awoke. My goal is to awaken the sleepers. One of the many insights I have inculcated is that without the equal growth of technology and spirituality our race is doomed. Without that balance, chaos will ensue. We are a young race and the young will make mistakes. As a child race, surprises are inevitable. Within a short time, some truly challenging ones will be upon us. I cannot predict what is coming. Timelines have changed, connected, and fused, causing great uncertainties. I am not a prophet. It does not take a prophet to see what is upon us. Much of this material has been "downloaded" to me and I share it with you.

It is up to all of us individually to elevate our minds and hearts. We must start with ourselves. We must question all thoughts and actions, always. We must be still to have clarity of thought. That is when true knowledge arises. Never maintain an opinion, for that stunts spiritual growth. Adopt a life of flow, the path of least resistance.

Some authors take fiction and weave it into reality in the minds of the readers. I, on the other hand, take a reality that seems like fantasy and weave it into a tapestry of truth. The truth is that this creation, this universe is far more complicated than we can understand and of which we are a critical component. What we experience as "Reality," is a mere subset of a much greater one, maybe even a simulation, possibly an experiment in free will.

A beginning is a most delicate matter. So, know that this is the year 2025. Time is perceived as speeding up by many and the world is changing fast, very fast. We all feel it. It feels dangerous, exciting, and somehow familiar. A collective Déjà vu perhaps. It is my fondest hope that I can bring some clarity as to why things are the way they are, to introduce the unbelievers and the fence sitters a personal and hopefully uplifting narrative so we can go into a future all being on the same page, working together, hand in hand, as one tribe. The tribe of humanity.

INTRODUCTION

There is no beginning and there is no end. Those are illusions. There is no past, there is no future, there is only the eternal now. How can a finite mind understand the infinite? There is only the unfolding of the illusion of time, which is the stage on which we play. And plays are stories. Some exciting, some not, but they happen none the less. Stories untold, stories unshared, may become a burden to the one who does not share. The eternal now is a delicate time. It is the razor's edge that we all must live, the balance of constant decisions. On one side fate, and the other side the gift of free will.

Allow me to introduce myself. In this present incarnation on this big, beautiful ball, I was given the name Stephen. I grew up in a prominent southern city to a middle-class nuclear family. It was a family that was mostly functional with a

Baptist upbringing. My paternal grandfather was a hellfire and damnation Baptist preacher who in his later years formed a mission to help wayward, indigent men traveling the rails. Many suffered from undiagnosed PTSD from WWII. My father was a WWII veteran that made a good middle class living selling insurance. My mom had a productive secret life. Besides being an incredible mom, after her home duties she was involved with many altruistic endeavors from PTA president, garden club, her church functions and work for Youth Home, a place for young people in need of a helping hand. She was heavily involved in the early era of the civil rights movement in the late 1950's. I was the youngest of three sons, learning from both of my brothers, I benefited in wisdom from their Erreur des Freres; their mistakes in life. I am retired now but wore many hats through my career years. I was a professional photographer, documentary film producer, audio and video contractor, copier tech, and computer and network analyst. I acquired a degree in electronics design and implementation. As I look back on my life, I have had a very interesting life but not in the conventional sense. In that conventional sense I used to think it was average, no longer. I came to realize I had been given an incredible gift of insight into the clockwork of the universe. As I have compiled my experiences, I came to realize it has been an extraordinary story. Firstly, I must declare that I am not a believer, I am, however, an experiencer. I do not believe everything I see or hear. I am skeptical of many stories I see online. They must have a logical premise, at the least they must pass my b.s. meter. There are many charlatans and deceivers and I have met my share. I have also met some individuals who have inspired me to come forth and share these experiences. I have often wondered what I could do to contribute something to the collective wisdom of mankind. I sense I have been protected from harm by forces unseen but often felt and I am eternally grateful. I have discovered that not only places on this planet can attract so-called paranormal phenomenon, but that individuals have the same capability to do so as well. Since the Covid-19 pandemic I have felt strongly compelled to document everything of possible interest. Honestly, I do not know how long we have before the great awakening will occur. As you well know, the world is rapidly changing and I fear for our species.

Everything you read in Part One is true, every single part. I have had other experiences that were important to my spiritual growth but they are scattered and do not necessarily cohere with the contents of this document. Some will be mentioned later.

The very first question you should be asking is where do I derive my authority on these subjects? That is a valid question especially with this material. In our society today we earn our authority in three basic ways.

One: We attend and earn grades by the judgements of so-called authorities and eventually degrees from schools, colleges, universities, and special training. In academic societies this is the conventional method. It is a good method. However, it is always limited to what scholars have discovered before and submitted their findings. It is not always first-hand knowledge. If a former scholar has made conclusions about a particular subject, it is either correct or not. That is why we peer review a work. Hopefully with rigorous testing a conclusion is met by the one's peers. This method is based on the logic of deduction. A general premise or rule that reaches a specific conclusion. This method works best for the left brain of an individual. This is classified as objective learning.

Two: Method two is experience. Some would say one is a graduate of HK University. The University of Hard Knocks. A University for Trades. Getting in there and working with one's hands and brains. Getting dirty and beat up a few times. It is a valid method of learning and becoming an expert in one's trade. Living the experiences. It often uses the right brain and uses the logic of induction. Inductive logic starts with specific and general observations and reaches a conclusion(s) based on patterns. This form of reasoning is opposite of deduction but just as valid. The right brain sees patterns where deduction breaks systems down, inductive logic sees whole systems. This is subjective learning.

Three: The superior method - one and two combined are the superior method. It is lived and is first-hand knowledge. This has been my experience through life. One often makes mistakes along the way but it also contributes to the learning process. My authority comes from both. I use both sides of my brain. I use both deduction and induction. Both subjective and objective learning. For example, I have been told that I am an artist, I like the liberal arts but technical endeavors as well. I am as comfortable at painting as I am fixing a computer. I have a degree in electronics, yet I love painting, woodworking, and cooking. I can see a system of interconnected sub systems in one vision. I very often build a thing using only the vision of that thing in my head. I rarely use blueprints because it is fully envisioned in my head. I am no more intelligent than the average person yet because I utilize both sides of my brain, I may seem more intelligent than I truly am. This has been so since I have been using a device called Questor. Which is a brain hemisphere synchronizer. I will elaborate further on. In my personal experience and viewpoint this is the method that all humans should use but we do not. With training all can achieve this method. We were never designed to use only one side of our minds. Without the training and use of both hemispheres of our brains we will always be only half as good as we could be. Another way of perceiving the total hemisphere perception is this. The left brain concentrates on, say a cherry blossom as a single flower that one might examine and judge it as flawed and that none can ever be completely flawless yet the right brain simply perceives that all cherry blossoms as perfect. The same goes for snowflakes and every creation as well. The left brain loves to divide the whole and the right brain embraces the whole.

With all this in mind it still comes down to whether you believe me or not. That is your choice and I will abide by that choice. Even if you do not believe or agree with me, I hope you will glean from this work a new vision of possibilities.

Part One of this document is chronologically based. Added is the subject matter for each pertinent year of my life when it involves unusual events. So, you can read and hopefully learn and enjoy or if you find the subject unsuitable then feel free to skip to the next chapter. The second section is what has been downloaded and /or given to me by powers way above my intellectual pay grade. It also contains a guide to begin to understand what has happened and what is really happening on this planet. This document is class level of Reality 101. It is designed for all. You may find some material elementary. These materials reintroduce you to, and tie into more complicated issues. It is my fondest hope that your take away from this literary adventure is a better understanding of yourself, the real you, of the world and why it is what it is, and what our place is in this thing called reality. It is your choice to take the blue pill of conformity and things will stay the way they have always been or your choice to take the red pill and take a trip down the rabbit hole, through a wonderland of possibilities, and realities untold. Even if you do not believe any of it is true I hope it will inspire you to learn more and give you hope for the future of us all. If you have your own story and you have not shared it with anyone, I hope this document will give you the courage to do so. The world needs to know what is occurring now whether it wants to or not. May you all have courage in all your endeavors.

From the beginnings of our current civilization that began sometime after twelve thousand years ago we humans have been traumatized so acutely from events so horrific that we suffer even today, not only from collective PTSD but from collective amnesia. Twelve thousand years ago the world was in total chaos known now as the Younger Dryas period and it came very close to being an extinction level event for mankind. This period is the time of Noah, the latest of many extinction level events. The peak of which we know today as the Biblical Flood. For those who do not know or believe the Bible there are many cultures around the world that have flood stories from this time. Humanity was nearly wiped out, creating the great loss of ancient wisdom and technology. Entire civilizations and cultures were destroyed. When technology was destroyed there was very little information left to rebuild again to the same level that was lost. We reverted to a stone age level and in that loss, we forgot our past and or history of what was before the flood. Thus began "the Great Amnesia."

We have lost the knowledge of our true incredible heritage and that knowledge has been cleverly and secretly replaced with a false reality of thought control and fear. We sank from intellectual heights only dreamed of today, to a new normal of savagery, greed, and fear.

The domination of a monetary society has rendered the masses to the level of soulless, economic slavery. A system of control that only a few through the centuries have known the full extent of its brainwashing, wealth, and power. It began as ruthless lords and kings with armies at their disposal that created kingdoms and divided the masses into tribal systems using fear to subdue any resistance from within and without. This system was justified by the rulers of that terrible time to secretly gather among themselves all the power and wealth they could. This system continues today and whether we like it or not this system is continuing to gain even more control, for men lust for power most of all. There have been fleeting moments of freedom from tyranny such as King John of England signing the Magna Carta and the creation of the new world specifically the United States of America and the destruction of the Berlin wall. These fleeting moments of freedom's expression are only won by the movement of the collective will of a society to move in certain directions.

Subtly and inexorably, we are now evolving into a fusion of cybernetics and flesh, of Artificial Intelligence (AI) and total control, a dystopia not unlike the movies that have warned us of this frightful vision.

This is a big world, yet, at the same time it is for all intent a spaceship isolated in the dark, cold, recesses of a galaxy isolated in a huge void, among trillions of other galaxies, that is being ravaged to fulfill the disposable needs of modern society, to be discarded in a very short time to then be replaced with new polluting toys that appease our boredom and simultaneously poisoning our environment and ourselves. We purchase things to fill the hole in our souls that we all have and do not know it. We buy new things in the vain hope those things will make us feel fulfilled.

We feel fractured because we have lost our connection to each other and to The Source. Technology has and is continuing to control our collective awareness. All technology is a double-edged sword. We have a vast network of communications yet more isolated than ever before. This is the tiger that we have by the tail. We keep hanging on to the current civilizational model in desperation for if we let go the tiger turns on us and devours its fearful prey. We must find a sustainable economic system that benefits all, not just a powerful few. A sustainable world society, not a utopia, is feasible yet we go blindly about our business desperately hoping someone else will remedy our situation. The truth is only we the people must make the changes, the elites will not, ever.

But...there is an alternative, we have a choice. A hard one to be sure but one that will bring a new version of an ancient reality before the great chaos twelve thousand years ago. A reality that works in harmony with the earth, each other and even societies beyond this world. This is the beautiful lady, the hard-won lady but she is the only other choice. The choices we face are either the beautiful lady or the tiger. We have lived in a patriarchal society for twelve thousand years. It is time to rebalance the scales, not to swing all the way to the maternal side but to the balance point at the center. For that is the only way out. A society based on the balance of the masculine and the feminine energies. No other social structure will work to move our society forward in harmony with our planet and ourselves.

I have thought back through my years on this world feeling this terrible gnawing of the belief that I had lived a very common, average life, much wasted potential. Yet, I have had a life so bizarre, so amazing, so profound, that I was compelled to share it. I never quite understood what purpose I had or what was the reason for all these bizarre events. And then it materialized, this solid idea, this crystalline form in my mind, I had all these experiences, I think, to share them with you, so you and I could find a little hope in this insane world through the extraordinary events in my life. Events that showed me so much more than I alien electrogravitic craft, visions, reincarnation, Sasquatch, shadow people, invisible beings, greys, astral projection, information downloads, Near Death Experiences, and more, much more. I now understand that NOTHING happens without a reason. I have been shown that now is the time for this document to be given to you to make a choice in whether to believe or not, to give you hope that there is life beyond life, that there is intelligent life out there and that we stand at the threshold of an incredible future. A future of vast potential for all mankind not just a few. We must be brave. To paraphrase an extraterrestrial (ET) once said to Colonel Corso in his book *The Day After Roswell*, "There is a brave new world coming if you can take it."

NOTE: When I refer to the highest and exalted being in this document I use many names. It has had many names over the centuries. The names I use are: All that IS, the Creator, the Source, God, and IAM. It is the indescribable, the Unknowable, the Eternal Mind, and the Infinite One.

NOTE: Most of the material in Part Two is not new. Much is in fact ancient. The Universal Laws are from the very beginning of time and space. Some materials are new theories and treatise about current conditions.

PART ONE

INTRODUCTION

In the early years of my life, I was just like most young boys. Went to school, went to church, feared The Bomb, and was growing up making my way through the mysteries of life. I had many neighbors that were around my age and we mostly played in a very different fashion than kids play today. We would always play outside playing army, Kick the Can, Simon Says, or ride our bikes from the time we got home from school until it was dark, or until our mom's called us home for a hot meal, then it was off to our bedrooms to do our homework. The climate was cooler then, so we had large amounts of snow in the winter, and warm and wet summers. It was a good time to grow up. In the fifties the nation was in a cold war with the Union of Soviet Sociality Republics (USSR) but it did not affect us directly. We cared only about having fun playing in the creek, building tree houses, making skateboards and go carts out of old metal skates. We would get into fights then make up as if nothing had happened. I remembered loving the sound of a propellor plane going over my house as I would lay in the front yard with my eyes closed without a care in the world. At the age of five my life was about to take a long detour into the strange, the unknown and a world of infinite possibilities. What was about to happen would change the way I perceived what we commonly and naively call Reality. What we humans experience as Reality is a mere shadow, a subset of a much greater and more complex Reality. A Reality that we can explore together. All I ask is that you open your mind to a greater Reality, a Reality that is our inheritance, a gift of God to let us play, to learn the responsibility of free will. Even if you just play along, suspend your disbelief in infinite possibilities come with me and just be comfortable in your reality. Believe what you will, I cannot force you to believe any of this document. None the less, it is as real to me as your reality is to you. This is the beginning of my journey to where I reside today. Come along on a strange ride.

Accompany me for a while and take a very deep dive into the strange manifestations of this beautiful creation, the universe, while sitting comfortably in your favorite chair.

In this section I will endeavor to describe and elaborate on what I believe what happened in each year of my life in Part One. With each of these events I learned something I believe is of great importance and relevance to what is happening on this planet and to our civilization at this time. How we all consider these experiences to be real or not, in the scheme of things it simply matters not. I was skeptical of these types of experiences that I read about in books and the news just like you until they happened to me.

The universe plays its own games and we are totally subject to the rules of those games, or are we? We can and do mold our reality to our will, but, within the confines of universal laws, we just do not realize it. Remember this, "All is Mind."

In our society we consider that there are two "Realities," one that occurs outside our skin and the other, that which occurs inside our skin. The outside reality stimulates our nervous system, feeds us information about what is happening in our vicinity. Is there danger, is it pleasant, what events are happening at this moment, what do you see, hear, taste, feel, and smell? These are sensations that are sent to our brain as impulses of electricity and INTERPRETED by the brain as outside events. Thoughts, feelings, and emotions are events that occur in our brains are also INTERPRETED the same way. So, in fact we now know that outside stimuli are impulses created by the brain and thoughts, feelings and emotions that are also created internally by the brain in the same way. In fact, all activity in the brain are electro-chemical waves interacting with each other in very specific ways. The flow of information from the outside mingles and fuses with our internal information creating new waves of thought. These waves start from specific points of nerves entering the brain depending on the type of stimuli. Say millions of impulses come from the optic nerves and thousands come from the auditory nerves this would create a flood of interference waves not unlike two children throwing pebbles in a lake close to each other. One child is the optic nerves and the other child is the auditory nerves. When the pebbles (nerve impulses) hit the water (cortex) they create (ripples), complex wave/information or interference patterns which creates memories, actions, and thoughts of a complex synthesis of sound and light mimicking the external and internal experience but they are not "real" they are created in the brain. Then feelings, emotions and memory are all a way of reacting to the original stimuli. As you realize, this is extremely complex and happens literally in the blink of an eye. If you could watch this miracle happening, after the impulses had left the nerve entry into the brain, once the waves interfered with each other, you would lose the ability to tell the difference looking at the wave patterns which were external or internal stimuli. Thus, in the brain, the outside world and the internal world dissolve into waves that function the same. Our brains create and experience the world through waves of information.

In the act of seeing this wave function of the brain both internal and external "Realities" are equally valid. This is especially true with dimethyltryptamine (DMT), a powerful hallucinogen where most outside stimuli are suppressed and the internal stimuli are extremely enhanced. DMT produces such a powerful internal experience that most users are convinced the drug is a gateway to other dimensions not hallucinations at all. I will go further into this subject a little later. So, for now let us go into the experiences I had through the years and see what we can learn from them.

PART ONE

STRANGE MEMOIRS
My Life by Year

FIVE years

Real Event

Out of Body Experience

When I was five, my two older brothers and I would play a game. They would have me sit on their feet while one or the other would lay on their backs with legs coiled up to launch me into space. This was the era of Sputnik, rockets, and astronauts. I loved the astronauts. At that time the astronauts were testing the X-15 rocket plane. I thought it was the most beautiful machine I had ever seen. So, my brothers were my rocket and I was going into space about two feet into the air. It was fun for a five-year-old. I never made it into orbit but, it turns out I went further than any astronaut would ever go.

You see, I died.

It turns out that I was launched in the wrong direction. My brother's calculations were a little off vector.

I tumbled to the ground and slammed the back of my head onto a rock. I learned my first rule of physics. I discovered that gravity is a bitch! It must have rattled the part of my brain that keeps me breathing. All I remember is a terrible pain and the jolt, like a bolt of electricity through my head, then black.
Then a most extraordinary thing occurred.
I was then watching my mother frantically carrying me toward the

house. She was crossing the upper terrace yard and down the stairs to the patio below. She looked terrified and apparently, she thought I was dying or already dead. I was being carried and not aware of it yet I was watching her from another place in the yard. Then I can only surmise "I," my consciousness was outside of my physical body. I was not afraid or even concerned. It felt somehow "normal."

I remember next the terrible headache. I could hear voices from far away and a high-pitched whine. The whine was drowning out the voices but they got louder and clearer. I then realized I was retreating through a tunnel looking back where I was coming from. The more I retreated in the tunnel the more my head hurt. The tunnel was very bright beams of light but warm and comforting and dividing the light, areas of darkness. Scary darkness. As the tunnel slowly faded the voices got louder and clearer. The intense whine receded. It was my mom and dad and Dr. Henry. I was coming back. I was aware of lying on my back on my parent's bed. I was looking up at all my family and Dr. Henry when he declared I would be all right but they would have to keep me awake to prevent me from going into a coma.

It turns out I had stopped breathing almost immediately after hitting my head. Mom had to do CPR to keep me alive until the doctor arrived. Mom had given me life twice, once in birth and she breathed life into me for a second time. It seems I had an OBE. An "Out of Body Experience."

She told me many years later that she had just watched how to perform an early version of CPR just a few days before the accident. Lucky for me. There are no coincidences!

The term NDE is a term I personally do not recognize. A "Near Death Experience" or NDE implies that a person does not completely die. If your consciousness separates from your body then you are dead. You are either alive or dead, one cannot be both unless you are Schrodinger's cat! If you are a physics nerd you will know what I mean. If one's heart stops and has no brain activity then one is dead. Period! When people say they have died and returned from a death state a large percentage were revived by medical intervention and they probably would not have survived without that intervention. They had an "Out of Body Experience" or OBE not an NDE and returned to the living. In the event of the body being unable to contain the soul any longer that is death but it is possible to be in a state where one is at minimum capacity, heart rate, brain activity then a coma can occur. The soul may or may not leave the body in a coma but it is a valid but a quasi-state of being. The experience I had when I was five was that I had quit breathing which triggered an OBE that I experienced as watching my mom carry me from the yard while "I," my consciousness was standing in another location as my mom revived me by artificial resuscitation measures. So, for a brief period I was dead. Seeing the classic "Tunnel of Light" I remember being returned from somewhere because I was retreating through the tunnel of light not moving into it.

For those who fear death, it may be terrifying before the instant of death but from then on, it is very easy. Some do not even know they have passed over such as those that have an auto accident. Carol, my friend, who knows much more about these subjects than I, once said "Death is sometimes easier than falling off a log." Some if not most are not even aware they have passed on. So please do not despair, it is inevitable and it's part of life. No one can change that. All things MUST change form at some point; stars die and even the universe dies, sort of. More on that in Part Two.

EIGHT

Real Event

A Night Encounter

I was, at this time in my life, a sickly child. I was afflicted with everything from colds to immune disorders. At one point I was home from school with growing pains in my legs so bad I had to pull myself across the floor on my elbows. At one point I had something that resembled leukemia, my parents were very scared of course, but they never said anything as to not scare me as well. It turned out all right as you can see. The confused doctors could never figure out what was wrong. It turned out it was an unknown virus with symptoms that resembled mononucleosis. In my research I found that other children who were at this age and who had similar experiences as I was having had unknown viruses. I had countless nose bleeds at this time in my sleep from unknown causes.

A year or so before this time my middle brother started swimming on a competition team for the Boy's Clubs of America. I was "encouraged" to participate as well. That means I was told to do so. It was just okay at first, but then I found out that I was a natural and I began to like it. Being a Scorpio, water is my element. I feel totally comfortable in water even today. My life, however, was about to change drastically.

A few months after I had started swimming, Steve J., my best friend at the time, invited me over to his house to camp out in his back yard. We went to church together and attended the same school. His backyard was totally enclosed in white lilacs that are invasive bushes, which love to grow along fence lines, formed a visual barrier. This campout occurred on a Saturday night in July of 1961. It was a warm night with a clear sky. We did not have a tent so we slept on old army cots from his dad's army days. They had that old mildew smell. The fact that we camped out this way left us exposed to the open sky. The crickets serenaded us all night. We had no fire, just the stars and the lightning bugs to keep us company, and it was too hot to sleep.

We talked for a long time, laughed, and giggled most of the night. I am estimating now that around 3 a.m. the crickets that had serenaded us all night suddenly stopped. It became dead quiet. There was not even a breeze. I saw it first, then Steve J. was gasping at what was moving toward and directly over us. The craft must have been in stealth mode. It was totally silent and had very dim lights. As it moved it covered the stars in shadow and we could tell its shape was round. The crazy thing was I was not scared at all; I was in awe, and I knew what it was seems as if it was familiar somehow. It came from the south southwest. All we could do was stare in silence. The feeling that I had was just pure, childlike wonder.

It was a circle of dim red light like a neon tube with a dim green light in the center. It was barely visible. Our child's minds simply could not believe what we were seeing. It was huge. It was 50 feet in diameter, at least. It floated about a hundred feet up and it moved like a balloon on a light breeze would do. Then…. it was gone, just gone. Winked out, it was there then it was not.

The crickets tentatively serenaded us once more; the threat had passed.

Steve and I just stared silently at each other, so dumbstruck, so shocked nothing we could have said could have made it feel more real, more fantastic.

The left brain in my head took over. Logic took over, so of course it was a helicopter, what else could it be right, a flying saucer? BWAHH No way. Yet, a helicopter makes a lot of noise. It would have awakened the whole neighborhood. Scared the shit out of everyone. At that time there were no helicopters in my city and this was 1961. We did not have one until the late seventies. I remember not talking anymore. Suddenly realizing we were tired, we went to sleep. I woke up and it was daylight, about mid-morning. Mom picked me up after we had breakfast. It was typical summer morning and we were happy. Everything was normal again but, then again it wasn't. We did not speak about that July night at all ever again. For an eight-year-old boy I now find that very odd. Sadly, Steve J. and his family moved away soon after and I have never heard from him again. I would like to have spoken with him to see what became of his experience.

On that following Monday night my brother and I went to swim practice. After I awhile, I was sitting, resting with my legs straight out. I noticed something on the outside of my left calf. Midway between my knee and ankle was a large scab. Being exposed to water it had softened up. I picked at it of course and as I did the scab came off. It did not hurt and it did not bleed. It just opened up. I got up from my rest and had to swim laps again. I finished and went back to examining my leg again. The swirling water had cleaned out the wound. There was no bleeding at all. I looked down into it as best as I could. What I saw startled me. It went deep, there was meat like raw steak and there were red things and blue things. At the bottom looked like a freshly cleaned bone, still pink from the blood inside. My God that is my leg bone, arteries, and veins!

My leg had been cored out like an ice core drilled out of the Antarctic ice. I felt sick and scared. What happened to me?

I did not realize until years later that after our encounter my health had improved dramatically. I did not put the two together until recently. I was now a very athletic teenager, strong and in perfect health. Ever since that time my immune system has been very good. Did something happen to me that night?

Many years later while reading various books of people's experiences with "The Visitors." The people in most cases had no idea of what was happening to them after the visitors, when they would find strange marks on their bodies in various locations, what are now referred to as "Scoop" marks. Some had unknown illnesses associated with their encounters. Of the ones I read about most had found the scoop marks on their legs. They had no idea what they were or how they got there until they put the pieces of their experiences together like I had to. I can only guess what the scoop marks are. I presume for tissue samples and genetic marking of the individuals the "Visitors" were interested in. Some experiencers claim they were told by their abductors that they have been tracing genetic family lines for thousands of generations presumably to get specific traits the abductors were wanting for reasons unknown, possibly for breeding stock or the abductees had certain abilities unknown to themselves. Almost universally alleged abductees report missing time in abduction scenarios. Many abductees claim they were first taken around the age of eight. In this experience I had no way of gauging time without clocks or wristwatches, remember, back then, we had no cellphones. At this point I can only presume I had missing time just long enough for the visitors to do whatever procedures they had to do to me, and probably Steve as well. From my point of view the entire event only took seconds from sighting to the craft vanishing. I may have been on that craft of hours; I have no idea. I just remember waking mid-morning, nothing unusual. Putting the pieces together, it seems these "Visitors" can control the flow of time. They can expand a few minutes of our "time" into hours on the craft. It is possible that time passes slower on board the craft and to our time awareness only minutes pass. Maybe it is far more complex. Unlike many who were and still are traumatized by their abductions I was fortunately not. I may have been "controlled" mentally as to reduce the trauma. I only remember flashes of things over the years that I did not understand at the time.

As I mentioned before, I was a sickly child and recently, I have found out that many abductees have had strange illnesses after their abductions. Could these illnesses be linked to extraterrestrial pathogens or inoculations?

FIFTEEN

Real Event

Second UFO Sighting

In my fifteenth year my parents, my middle brother and I moved into our new home. It was a big, beautiful two-story colonial home.
For a 1967 house, it had all the latest conveniences. Mom designed many of the features. It had four bedrooms, three baths and about 3 thousand square feet. It was on top of a ridge overlooking the Arkansas river and was the first of many new very nice homes in the housing addition. For a while we were all alone in the woods. Many strange things were going to happen in and around that house.

Keith W., a friend I went to school with, who lived a few blocks away in an already established neighborhood. He was smart, funny, and wild. We had good times together. A little over a year after we had moved, in the winter of 1968, Keith had been visiting my place and we were going to his house to have dinner. His parents were having guests over and I was Keith's. We had walked about a block from my house when we saw it. We had a clear view of the sky. The leaves had fallen and most of the trees had been removed to build another house. The stars were out and bright. One was brighter than the rest. It started moving over the lights of downtown to the east of us. We were on top of a hill so we had a great view. At first it moved slowly, oh heck, it's just a plane, boring! Then suddenly, it shot down to the ground like it was going to crash into the downtown area.

Stopped instantly, whoa, then goes into a wild zigzagging path all above the city. It moved like an insane flying insect. No human alive could have withstood the gravity forces of this craft, if it was a craft. It could have been an alien drone. It certainly was not of human construction. The path it made was extremely defined, sharp starts and stops with incredible sharp narrow angles. It paused for a second then shot straight up and disappeared at astounding speed.

We ran to his house, crashed through the door and we excitedly told everyone that we had just seen a UFO. There was a group for dinner of maybe a dozen guests that arrived before us. There was a pregnant pause, then a snicker, then crickets. Everyone went back to their conversations like nothing happened except two crazy teens had just seen a UFO. SURE!

We learned that night to keep our mouths shut like most people do.

This was the second time I had seen an unidentified flying object (UFO), unidentified anomalous phenomena (UAP), or possibly an NHICC or non-human intelligently controlled craft (NHICC). It was awesome to see this object moving in the sky with such deliberate maneuvers and speed, also to experience the sighting with a close friend to confirm the sighting. With its erratic yet controlled movements, the object must have been seen by many people downtown. Yet again, now knowing human behavior better, people going about their busy lives do not look at the sky much anymore and I find that tragic and sad. Living in large metro areas, we have ignored the skies and lost another connection to our true understanding of what our reality truly is.

Take the time to go out to a dark area in the countryside, take your wives or husbands, significant others, children, friends or just yourself and look up and fully experience the cosmos, the Milky Way, the moon, see it with your inner feelings and know that you are a part of something truly incredible, wondrous and exciting called the Universe and life itself which is sadly and tragically taken for granted by most human beings living today.

Life is a GIFT, a gift billions of years in the making with the life and violent death of gargantuan stars creating the elements that make up your body and the world that gives YOU life that in turn you may realize how special and precious life truly is.

SIXTEEN

Out of Body Experiences or Astral Projection

This sixteenth year would turn out to be a very eventful one as you will see. The vast majority of the populations of the western world have lost the understanding of the true nature of our being. As a whole we see only see the logical half. The world we live in is self-evident. The western world has mostly rejected the eastern religions and doctrines and are focused on materialism and capitalism. The fundamental eastern philosophies revolve around the concept of a soul that evolves to rise to higher levels of awareness and adopt it into the daily lives whereas western religions rely upon an emissary, the church, completely decoupling from the soul's responsibility to evolve to a higher state.

I believe we lost our spiritual knowledge as a racial memory after the Flood, the Younger Dryas period, approximately 12,000 years ago. To state it simply, we are "Soul Blind." Blind to the fact that we are more than just physical beings. The following are my experiences with the astral body or "Soul." It is so fantastical to modern man that we now refuse to believe it is our true nature. Thankfully, many are now experiencing what I experienced so many years ago when it was virtually unknown to the common man.

It was now 1969, a time of exploration and revolutionary changes in many areas of society. My middle brother had been expelled from his first semester for playing a practical joke on a classmate whom he did not like at a Louisiana college. So, he had to stay back home until he could be enrolled in a state university. Because his expulsion had been so devastating, he started his journey into an expanded frame of mind. I remember sitting in his room talking about things, I do not remember what about but during one of our conversations he just started staring at me in puzzlement like a dog does with their cute little head bob when they are confused. He said "you have a white halo around your head" then he went back to talking about something. A few days later he handed me a book. It was called *Practical Astral Projection* by YRAM, I supposed was probably a pseudonym, YRAM, Mary spelled backwards. I was totally fascinated by it. How was this even possible? Your soul leaving your body at will? Fantastic? As it turned out it was quite real.

If you have never heard of it, Astral Projection is a technique and a practice of separating "You" or your "energy body," your soul, from your physical body. I found out it has been practiced for thousands of years by people in secret societies, shaman, learned men and priests of various beliefs and religions. At this time, I had never heard of astral projection. And growing up in the Bible Belt I am pretty sure no one I knew had either. I will get into this in depth in later chapters.

I am a slow reader but I read the book from cover to cover in 2 days. I was fascinated by the possibilities of what could be done with this knowledge. I could go anywhere not just on earth but beyond, way beyond. It would be like being invisible, and quite possibly travel through time as well. The night I finished reading I did the relaxation technique from the book's instructions, and I had results! I noticed my body started to vibrate like the hum of a loose connection on a stereo system. HMMMMM. It started to change, rising in pitch, and as it rose, I heard crackles and pops which I later surmised were my brains synapse breaking their electrical connections to my body. This was a strange new sensation, but it never hurt. As the pitch rose so high I could not hear or feel it but simultaneously, I felt as if my skin was peeling away. No pain but there was a feeling of peace and wonderment. Then a sensation no words can describe. I was out of my body. I freaked. I was in two places at the same time. This was beyond words and it was real!

What was strangest of all was that it felt natural as if I knew this sensation, it seemed familiar. My head was up and above my physical head and my right arm was up and out as well. What I was astonished to see was my right arm as if looking at an x-ray in florescent green. Bones, muscles, joints, everything that should be in my physical arm.

This was simply incredible. Then I panicked, SNAP, I, me, my soul, my astral body was within my organic body again. Fear snaps you back into the body.
Fear is an evolutionary adaptation inherited from species going back down toward the root species we came from to protect the life form from physical damage or death. Fear is a default response of the Default Mode Network (DMN) in the brain, occurring only in the biological form. It is the base form for the Ego body, the protector of our biological body. It prepares the body for the fight or flight situation. It stems not from the weakness of the person experiencing it, but is totally automatic.

Sometime later, a few months maybe, it was time to get back on the horse so to speak. At this time a storm came up with an impressive amount of lightning. It was a strange night to be sure. The air seemed electrified. I was going in and out of sleep when suddenly "I" was not in my bed, but I never got out of bed. "I" was standing in the hallway on the other side of my closed door. It was dark with flashes of lightning. Mom and dad were the only other people in the house at that time. Floating in the hallway about ten feet away were two orbs of light about ten inches in diameter, sort of a greenish white in color. For some reason I knew the orbs were my parents (souls?) but they must have been unaware of my presence because I asked them the next morning if they remember seeing me in the hallway that night, they did not and looked at me in a peculiar way and we went on about our business with no further discussion.

Again, one night "I" remember just "slipping" out sideways while lying on my side to the left. These experiences were becoming spontaneous. And then I saw the oddest thing. About six feet away was the lower half of a human torso. I "felt" this powerful presence as masculine. He had a bejeweled skirt made of a golden-colored metal like the skirts the Roman soldiers wore in battle. He imparted some knowledge to me with thoughts not words. Most of the information I do not remember. There were images, symbols and diagrams of almost incomprehensible detail and scope. I was informed that I would remember it over time. Over the years as I started to remember I had a faint intuition that the entity that visited me that night was someone from the ancient past or even the far future. I will explain in later chapters how and why that can be possible. I awoke refreshed.

Note: as of this writing it is 5.19.24. As I mentioned above, details of the download can be revealed over time. Just a few weeks ago I realized that the entity above may have been Thoth. He fits the profile of a deliverer of esoteric information and the teacher of those who seek knowledge. Thoth is believed to have been an actual person that is said to be an ascended master and immortal from the ancient past. In Greece, Thoth was known a Hermes, the deliverer of knowledge. A god of Egypt. More details about him in Part Two.

The Book of the Dead?

A Dream? Astral Experience?

A few months passed without incident. One night I had a most vivid dream experience, actually, it was more than vivid. It may very well have been an astral experience. I remember it well, walking on a path through the woods. It was a bright, beautiful day. Out of nowhere there was a young man who approached me on the path from the direction I was headed. He never told me his name and he seemed friendly enough. We had a conversation which I do not recall. Soon I began to feel he was too friendly. I remember him inviting me to see something wonderful. He asked me to follow him, reluctantly I did. I remember a castle in disrepair coming up before us. It looked ancient, walls collapsed, wet stones that smelled of long decay. As we approached, I noticed we were heading for what looked like a cave leading into and under the castle. I have no idea where this castle is located or even if it exists on earth at all. I "sensed" that it may be in Europe somewhere but as we approached, I started to feel an uneasiness about this place.

The closer I came to the castle the greater my anxiety became but my weakness of will and strength of curiosity got the better of me. As we entered the cave, I could smell something decaying and moldy, dank and drops of cold water dripped on me. This place was OLD. I followed him unsure of the situation into a great hall. It was about sixty feet by sixty feet wide and about a hundred feet high. It had arched openings at the top that provided light, but it was still dim. Birds nested and flew about above us. The puzzling thing in this hall was a very large pile of broken jagged rocks seemingly had fallen from the structure above long ago. The broken stones rose about thirty feet to a peak in the middle of the room, sort of the rough shape of a pyramid. At the top was a platform with a podium. Upon it was a large book placed with great care and reverence. The young man bade me up the rocks to see this "wonderful" object. We came to the top and stood before the book. I was apprehensive. A book of large proportions about six inches thick by eighteen inches high by about fourteen inches wide lay before me.

Again, he bade me to open it and read. I examined it carefully but did not touch it. As I delayed in my study the young man became insistent on me touching it and reading the book, his treasure. And then it struck me hard, now I was terrified.

What I perceived to be an evil creation made from the darkened stretched skin of human beings, bound in bone, and written in the blood of the innocent. This ornate book was fashioned by evil hands and was ancient. On the front was a carved bone relief of what looked like a left silhouette of a Satyr sitting on a toadstool playing a pipe. He opened it forcefully, his eyes full of impatience and anger. "Read it" he demanded as he slammed his finger onto a random page. I glanced at it but did not read it. At that point, in one leap, I turned and jumped from the top of the rocks to the stone floor and ran out as fast as possible. I awoke terrified and my heart pounded.

It was still Nineteen Sixty-Nine. What an incredibly intense year that was. It was a year of tumultuous change in our world, our nation, and our lives. The world was in flux like I have never known until these last few years. The nation was about to tear itself apart over civil liberties, the war in Viet Nam, the hippy movement, psychedelic drugs, women's liberation movement, art, music, the sexual revolution, riots, and the first steps by mankind on another planet, our moon. One could argue that it was the most revolutionary time of the twentieth century, not because of war but the massive volume of societal changes that took place in that single year.

It was also an incredible year for me not only externally but internally as well. Just a few months before I had asked the Universe to teach me its secrets. My wish was to be the beginning of my quest. My oldest brother took me to see Curtis, a Tarot card reader. In my reading of the Tarot, the card known as "The Star" came up but also drew my attention. "The Star" signifies hope, faith, and spiritual connection. Curtis said soon I would learn about many wonderful things. I literally wished upon a star! I would say my wishes were answered with my strange experiences through my life. Curtis did not have a blue dress and wings but I did perceive him to be much like a wizard of age's past. He reminded me, as I grinned, of the Greek, Diogenes who wandered, always looking for an honest man.

You see, it was a major turning point for me in the way I perceive everything, the way I am showing you (hopefully), now. I have learned that perception is extremely important in shaping our internal and external worlds. It is a two-way lens to perceive the internal and the external worlds. It is the molder of our reality and the potter's hands of the mind's eye. Our thoughts color and distort our view of the world, and the world reflects that back to us. I learned that reality is plastic, it is not set in stone. I know that must sound ridiculous but to experience this new reality one must open their mind to possibilities as if it is a game, a game you can change by changing your thoughts.

Understand that just by reading this document you have started to change your perception of reality, you have taken the first step into a whole new world. That is the power of thoughts and words. More on this in part two.

Astral Travel Event

The Andromeda Trap

Sometime months later, asleep, I felt a strong pull upward and outward. I rose out of my body and above the house. High in the sky I started to accelerate into space. Faster and faster, I flew, I looked back and saw the earth retreat into darkness. I went passing the surrounding stars in a blur as I shot out of the Milky Way galaxy. I was moving now though intergalactic space. It was a feeling of freedom I cannot express with words. There was a light ahead, steady in front, approaching it. It looked much like the Andromeda galaxy. It was! It was shaped as I remember.   A galaxy 2.5 million light years away and our closest galactic neighbor. In about 4.5 billion years it will collide with the Milky Way and the two will in a few more million years become one in a slow-motion dance of destruction and creation of a new and larger galaxy. A child galaxy. As I approached Andromeda I was slowing down and being drawn in toward the dense inner mass of the spiral arms close to the super massive black hole at the center. I descended to the surface a verdant planet circling what looked to be a main sequence star much like our sun. The vegetation was green but different and the environment was tropical. I noticed something black on the horizon. It was hard to tell for the haze of moisture in the air. It looked to be at least twenty miles away. I had to know what was going on so I decided to launch out toward it. As I approached, I began to see the scope of this thing and more details revealed themselves. It was huge! If you had an old, pitted iron cauldron and turned it upside down and buried it halfway, and the cauldron was a couple of miles high and at least twenty miles wide you would get the idea of the size. It was sometime later I arrived at its surface. It was just black, ancient, and deeply pitted. No noise but a breeze in the foliage. I reached out to touch it and as my hand made contact, yet it did not. My hand passed through it with a slight humming and mild electric shock. I paused, feeling it was safe.

I passed into the surface and once inside I was standing in a great circular hallway that was just on the inside stretching out to the left and the right. I walked for what seemed like hours moving toward the center. There were miles of halls, but I found no rooms. It was a labyrinth of halls. Soon I heard voices, I approached cautiously. What I saw was truly disturbing. People, human beings were chained to the walls of the hallways with heavy chains. Naked and filthy they were paying no attention to me as they went about their business. Their business was having sexual intercourse, drugs, alcoholic drinks, and any debauchery you can and cannot imagine. I sensed it was a trap, fly paper for lost souls never to leave again. Some would suggest this was a Hellscape. I was truly saddened by their inability to leave, you see, it was not just their chains that bound them it was their lusts for pleasure, only their pleasure, their greed of it. They had trapped themselves willingly. This went on for what seemed like an eternity of miles. Many millions were here if not billions. The sounds of their weeping tore me apart. I moved on ever toward the center that I felt the inexorable pull. At the end I came to a great door, ever open like a sticky trap for the unwary, pulling me inside toward inevitability.

The trap was now set, circular, and about the size of a football field. The ceiling was high above and dark, cold, and depressing. In the center stood a three-foot column as if it just poured out on to the floor and frozen in place. Placed upon it was a glowing crystal ball about one foot in diameter. To my amazement it spoke. With the most seductive voice I have ever heard it asked me my name. I did not reply. This was no human intelligence; this was an ancient being of vast intellect and power. I could feel its power. Merely being in its presence was terrifying. It was beyond malevolent. I asked who it was, and it laughed and said, "I am no one. I am the unnamed.

However, I am merciful and giving. If you bow down and worship me, I will give you the keys to all you desire, the knowledge of all things.' I realized what it was and I then said; "I know what you are and I will have no part of it." Knowing if I accepted its offer, I would never leave that place again. My body would probably have been found dead in my room that morning from unknown causes. This may be the reason many pass in their sleep. At that moment the crystal ball lit up to a blinding, bright red. At the same moment I felt another presence behind me. I turned to my left and looked up. I saw the red light from the crystal ball reflected in the opening eyes of a giant of a man hidden this whole time up in the darkness of the trap. I ran and I mean ran like a scalded animal. The giant was a least twenty feet tall. He had rage in his eyes. I had rebuked his master and that was not allowed here. He got close to catching me but for the fact here in this astral body I had no tiring muscles and could feel no pain, I passed through the wall and made it outside into the forest, safe. He did not follow maybe because he was trapped as well, possibly longer than the stars will shine. I woke, sat up in my bed and thanked God I was safe.

Bozo Nose

Astral Experience

During a night of that same year another event occurred. I became aware I was standing on a sidewalk that led to my old elementary school. I was very much aware I was in my astral body. Sitting a few feet away from me was a bald man in a lotus position. He exuded a tranquil demeanor. He was there with me, yet he was not there. Oh yes, he was real, and he was at total peace, and in that peace, he was the still on the surface of a tranquil pond. I have no idea who he was, but I felt that he was aware of my presence but did not acknowledge me. It was dark of course but above me was a mercury streetlamp giving off its violet blue aura. This one was an extremely colorful display with what looked like threads of electric currents like tiny lightning bolts inside the aura. I felt no heat, humidity, cold or pain of any kind. I felt very much alive and peaceful. It was a beautiful experience.

Then things changed abruptly. I felt, sort of, that I was in a dream. The next thing I experienced was being on the roof of my house looking in my bedroom window on the second floor. At the same time, I was drifting through the window into my bedroom. My astral body automatically shifted to align with my physical body lying on the bed. As I drifted slowly down into my body, feet first then the rest of my astral form followed. The instant that my head started to merge I wanted back out and my astral body responded immediately and effortlessly. My astral body floated up by thought only and I was standing at the foot of my bed. This was incredible! I dared to turn around and look at my material body. I found my body sleeping peacefully. I was startled but not afraid this time. I was getting used to this now. It felt somehow natural. I turned back around and I looked at my hands and my fingers. They had tiny little lightning bolts like static electricity protruding from the tips. There was no pain. This was fun! I also noticed that they were coming off the end of my nose. To my astonishment it tickled and I thought about Bozo the clown reacting to something like this. I giggled with glee. Then I saw that there was an electric aura all around me, coming out of my entire body and the bodily protrusions were hot spots of concentrated electrical activity. One might ask if I can see, can I hear as well? What about touch, taste, and smell? I could hear a static-like noise as from a radio or television between channels. It is truly difficult to describe it. It would pop and crackle and sometimes it sounded like small wind chimes. Hearing, check. Sight, check. As for taste and smell? Smell yes, remember my excursion into the castle? Taste, I am not sure, but I would assume taste under the right circumstances would work as well. Now touch, that is a little trickier. Like in the ghost movies my hands would go through anything physical. But strangely I could stand on solid ground or the second floor of my home. I decided this was enough for one night and I thought I will go back into my body now. I merged with my physical body, and I was awake the entire time, excited, energized and I felt more alive than I had ever known in my sixteen years on this world. It opened my mind to the limitations of our race; how much we do not know and how much we have not been privy to. It was glorious, a triumph and this opened new ways of thought and becoming a full Human Being.

Looking back and learning new things about other's experiences, electricity, and biology, I am convinced that during puberty and the teen developing years that the human body is at its peak abilities to utilize these bio-energetic pathways in the brain/neuro-kinetic system and the hormonal output of these forces that exist naturally in the human body. So, it is imperative to start in puberty or even earlier to develop these abilities to reach their peak capacity extending through life.

One cool summer night of the same year I decided to open my window to let the southern breeze refresh my room. You might know how teen-age boys are? The window was designed as to allow a crack at the bottom and the top. Later that night I awoke to the terrifying sound of someone breathing in and out. Whatever it was it sounded large. I got up the courage to peak out from under the covers. I looked around, nothing but breathing in and out. My heart was pounding as I rose from the bed and looked around. My mom had installed roll up shades that the edges were tight up against the inside of the window frame. As the breeze came in the shade would blow in and when the breeze blew out the shade followed scraping against the wooden window frame. The window was breathing. My imagination had gotten the best of me that night but only that night.

I thought I would break any tension at this point because things are about to intensify from here on.

My Guardians and the Body Snatcher

Dream event/ astral event

Yet another night that same year I was dreaming of being at work at my job in a pizza restaurant, in the supply closet. I was standing on a creaky old stool to reach an upper shelf. As I was reaching for a box someone grabbed me from behind. It startled me enough to lose my balance and I fell backwards. There was a brief WHOOSH. At that point the "dream" instantly became an astral nightmare. Not of fearful things but of confusion, disorientation and by far the most painful experience of my life. Words simply cannot describe the agonizing pain. The closest I can get is this. Try to imagine being burned over your entire body, electrocuted, and every atom being ripped apart all at the same time. I could not black out from the pain and it was probably seconds but it felt like eternity. I realized I was back in my bed. I cried out for God to help me. Please help me. Instantly, I felt tender warm hands wrap around each of my upper arms. I looked to each side to see what had me so firmly yet merciful in their grasp. They looked like nuns with hoods over their heads but they were not nuns. I can only surmise that for their grace and their radiant, beautiful appearance that they must have been angels, maybe my guardian angels. I am not sure. They then grasped me hard and pushed equally as hard to force me back into my body. Why were they pushing me? I must have picked up on some form of information that these beings imparted to me. What I intuitively aware that something evil was trying to take possession of my body and as the "Angels" were "pushing" me back into my body, the entity passed through me and that was the incredible pain I felt. Our essences must have merged for a moment. As I rose up I was in pain that lasted for some time. Yes, God does answer prayers!

If that terrible pain is what resides in hearts of evil entities for the thoughts and evil acts, they have committed then I can be wary of them and guard against their attacks but I also feel compassion for the painful eternal existence they must endure in their private hell.

All these astral events were occurring during my middle teen years in the late 60's, a tumultuous time in

America. There being no internet, very few obscure writings that I could not get my hands on to read and living in the Baptist Bible Belt there was simply no one to confide in, no one that would even begin to understand what I was going through. I felt alone, concerned I was going insane and feeling vulnerable after these above-mentioned events. I reached out to a very few friends who looked at me as if I was insane. It is a very lonely feeling. For a very long time I gave up trying to explain what was happening. So, I understand what any of you readers may feel under the same type of circumstances. Do not be afraid now, humanity is awakening to these phenomena, so it is much easier to speak out. You just may find that there are now many people that have experienced what we have experienced but have not spoken out.

The Shadow Man???

Another entity was about introduce itself. On another occasion I remember being in "the Zone." That point where you are neither asleep nor awake. Scientists call it "a Hypnogogic State." It is a state that some believe powerful, realistic hallucinations can occur. It is very possible, regardless what science says, that the experiences can sometimes reach into our reality, not hallucinatory. It is also a state that one cannot move, usually. Honestly, I cannot say if it was real or not, but it certainly felt real and I was very much able to move. Very strange things can happen in this state. I felt a very strong presence nearby. In fear, I opened my eyes as I lay in bed and was greeted by an inky, dark hooded being, hovering only inches from my face. It was approximately 3 feet tall, reflecting no light, it even seemed to absorb light, it darker than the dark.

Floating above me, trapping me in the bed, under the sheets. I was terrified. Oh my God it had no face, no eyes yet I could feel its stare. I also felt curiosity, anger, loathing and even envy from it. I immediately grabbed what I could barely discern as its shoulders. It was black against the dark of the room. It had solid mass; however, I could not tell if this was a physical threat or an astral body threat. I remember fighting with it, punching it, and it hitting me. Yes, I felt pain. It dislodged from my grasp and it floated back in retreat and vanished. I remember my heart was pounding and I found myself standing on the bed, in a defensive position.

It was years before I was to hear of "Shadow People." Many, many thousands of people over the years have come forward with their experiences with these terrifying entities. Many will think these entities are hallucinations, but I assure you they are quite real.

Addendum: In my fifties, after my divorce, I was asleep with my partner at this time. I did not experience this because I was fast asleep, but her recollection of what happened one night has haunted me ever since. She remembered waking, feeling a presence in the room standing over her. She opened her eyes and standing only inches from her was a tall, shadow figure, wearing a broad-brimmed hat and a trench coat. She could not recall any other features, just shadow in the dark. She said it had no face yet she felt it was staring down at her. As she became terrified and waking me in the process, she turned back to look at him but he had vanished.

That morning, we got up and researched the internet for anyone experiencing anything like this. What we found was extremely troubling. It turned out many people around the world had experienced the same entity. He has been such a common experience, he was given a name, "Old Scratch." Another name he has been given is Lucifer. If "Old Scratch" is a hypnogogic hallucination it seems to be a universal one, but why the hat and trench coat, that is an identifier?

SEVENTEEN

A Shared Dream

Real Event and Lucid Dream Event

When I was seventeen, I was a sophomore in high school. I had made a new friend, Keith B. from Memphis, Tennessee. I had also graduated the previous spring from junior high school with two other friends, Lewis, and Mark. A few days before our experience the Lincoln Hotel in our city, had burned to the ground a few weeks before. It had been a well-known house of ill repute for many years. One night during the school year something happened that I cannot explain but it is along a similar path of my other high strange experiences, I found myself having what is now known as a Lucid Dream. I was walking among the burnt out remains of the Lincoln Hotel. There were piles of debris everywhere. In that lucid dream Mark and I were looking for the cash register to see if any cash had been left behind. Keith B. and Lewis were off doing something else at the same time.

Suddenly, out of nowhere a police car showed up. Mark and I were immediately spotted and were told to stand still with our hands up. The policemen approached us and asked what we were doing. Then they spotted the cash register. They handcuffed Mark and me for trespassing and as we were being led the squad car, I saw Keith and Lewis hiding. They had not been noticed by the police officers, and they got away. The next day at school I spoke with Keith and before I could tell him what I dreamed about he spoke first and mentioned he had a dream about us that same night. We four all had study hall that afternoon together and I asked Mark and Lewis if they had any dreams last night. Oh yeah, they did. Mark jokingly mentioned that he and I had been arrested going through a cash register while Lewis and Keith got away. I had not said anything of what I remembered about the dream yet. We all found out as the conversation revealed that we had the same dream that night and remembered it from our own points of view! I blew it off as a strange occurrence for many years.

There was no way at the time to compare it to anyone else's experiences.

I had at that time never heard of shared dreams until I saw a movie years later called *Explorers* with Ethan Hawke and River Phoenix. It was about some friends that have a shared dream about flying over gigantic circuit boards. They realized they were dreaming the same dream so they put their dream knowledge together and they create an anti-gravity bubble of energy that could transport them anywhere. They end up meeting an alien child. A fun and very revealing film from 1985. This phenomenon may be more common than I ever thought possible. Searching the internet, I found that 1 in 1000 people have shared dreams and have reported them to others. That is a very significant worldwide number. According to one site what I had with my three friends is now referred to as a "Meshing Dream." Who is to say that the people who have shared dreams with others they do not know in their lives but are complete strangers acting out parts in their dream? Who is to say that the people that populate our dreams are not real people dreaming their dreams and you might be their dream people? Who is to say that this is not a very common phenomenon for people all over the planet and possibly a very important component of our shared reality? The obvious conclusion is that both the dream world and the waking world are both real. We can all share the dream world and each other just as in the "real" world. A consensus dream reality? With my experiences described in this document with all these events in my life and of course all the combined experiences of people all over the planet does it really seem so far out of the realm of possibility? I think now that it is far more common than anyone realizes. The holographic universe model does not automatically rule shared or mesh dreaming out of the question, in fact it makes meshing dreams possible. As you are realizing, the world is a mysterious and wonderful place far bigger and varied than we ever thought possible. More about the holographic universe later in Part Two.

EIGHTEEN

Real Event

Impossible Beams of Light, third UFO

This eighteenth year turned out to be a terrifying one. On a hot summer late afternoon three friends, Steve B., Lindsey and Stan and I decided to drive up to a cleared area on top of a mountain overlooking the Arkansas

River below. You could see for miles looking toward the north and west. In that area below there is a mountain that looks like a small volcano, or at least I always thought it did. I remember driving around it at night about a year before. The brush in some places was on fire forming what looked like lava trails pouring down the mountain. It was beautiful.

My friends and I spoke of that and many other things that teenage boys talk about. Mostly I think the topics were girls, nerdy stuff... and girls. You get the picture. We talked for hours. It was getting late and the sun had already set. The afterglow was still hanging in the air when we decided it was time to leave. I was driving us in my car, an English Ford Cortina.

We had started home when we saw a strange orange light hovering over the river to our left about a mile away to the north. We could see it clearly because the trees had been cleared to build a home there. I stopped the car so we could watch it. We hung around for about twenty minutes out of pure curiosity. It was amazing and hypnotic. It had two search lights blazing down to the river. Two possible machines could look like this. One was a river barge, but they always had one light and barges did not glow orange. Two, it could have been a helicopter looking for something. The only problem was no official entity that had helicopters at their disposal at that time, in the state, except the military. Helicopters are not orange and, we could hear no noise whatsoever, except the crickets. There was no "chopper" sound at all. So, it could not be a helicopter. We still had our doubts about what it was and we watched it a little longer. We became bored with it because all it did was sweep the river with the lights. I have been known to pull off some practical jokes in my life, I like to shake things up for fun. At that point I decided to shake things up. I turned off the headlights and swung the car around to the left to align the car lights so they would hit this thing. I hit the lights, high beams, and all. I got its attention all right! It lit up immediately and turned very bright orange. We could see its details now. It was a disc about one hundred feet in diameter and about fifty feet above the water.

We could see its reflection on the water clearly. Still, it could have been a helicopter or so we thought. At this point it did something very strange. The beams of light did not just blink out. They RETRACTED! You could see the ends of the beams clearly. Light in our world just does not do that! Normally you can see the beam then it is gone. It does not retract like its being pulled back in. When the beams were retracted the disc lit up even more to a blinding light, flashed through the visible spectrum and started to rise away from the river, changed to white light, and shot straight up much faster than any rocket with no sound whatsoever. It disappeared into the night. It just blinked out. We looked at each other in total amazement and no one spoke about it again.

What we witnessed was so strange that it is hard to describe. The entire surface of the craft glowed a florescent orange as if it was painted in dayglow paint. It made no sound that we could hear--no rotor blades, no exhaust nor could we see control mechanisms. The two beams from this disc were short and wide angled and much brighter than the barge arc lights. I was very familiar with barges since I lived above a Lock and dam complex on the same river and saw them almost every night. Being very familiar with physics, these two beams did not conform to any known physics we common folk are aware of. They appeared much denser than ordinary light beams, they almost looked like a liquid. They had ends to them, truncated, and rounded off like the bottom of a water drop. I was scratching my head for weeks afterwards trying to figure it out. It was not till many years later, scientific journals described what it could have been, possibly a proton beam. It requires nothing less than a powerful proton accelerator to project protons into the air. Protons have mass unlike light and need many millions of watts of electrical power to produce a beam of this design and size. The protons are accelerated from a source and when they strike atoms of air molecules they produce a bright plasma glow. The greater the acceleration the farther the protons travel through air and since the center of the beam gets accelerated farther and the outer areas of the beam are less accelerated, the beam takes on a truncated or tear drop shape. If this was in fact a proton beam technology, with our level of knowledge today this would not only be impractical and incredibly expensive not to mention impossible for the early 1970's. So, this simply cannot be our human technology even today. So why go to all the trouble to produce a proton beam when conventional LED tech can be utilized. These beams of ??? are a much higher level of technology than we possess today. This craft and associated "light" beams seem as easy to produce for them as us turning on powerful LED headlights today on an automobile. It may be possible for us in a thousand years. Maybe. Unless some humans have access to this level of technology already. We shall talk more about this possibility in Part Two.

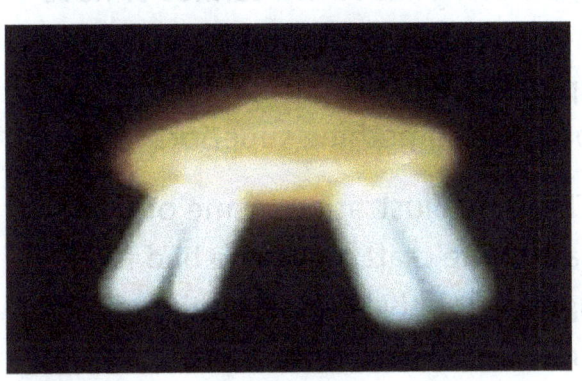

Tavernes, Var, France UFO | The UFO Database

This photo was captured in 1974 in Tavernes Var, France.[1] The craft we experienced had two beams of light not four. This photo was considered a fake at the time because of the truncated light beams could not possibly be real. With all my being I assure you the craft we saw was quite real. Among the many flaws of humans is in our hubris and ignorance, we assume that if we cannot or have not invented something then no other species could produce, let alone produce something superior.

This is an illustration by me of what we saw.[2] The craft may have had four lights but only two were utilized. The craft's glow was reflected on the water below.

Among the many flaws of humans is in our hubris and ignorance, we assume that if we cannot or have not invented something then no other species could produce, let alone produce something superior.

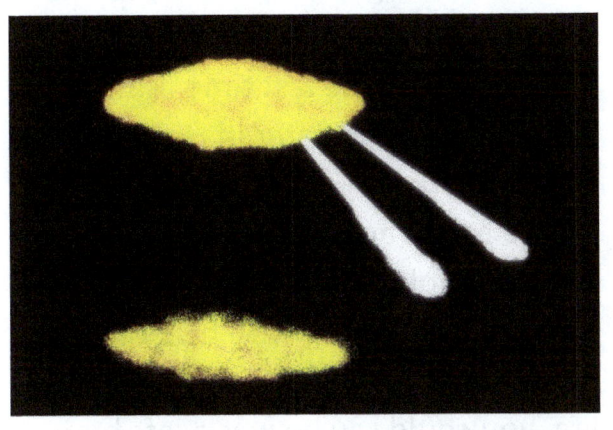

[1] Stockton, S.A. (1973) Drawing.

A Terrifying Intrusion

Real Event

It was summer of 1971, soon to be my senior year in high school. Life was good, I had girlfriends, I was active in school activities and doing ok in the grades department, I was a maverick at that age. Funny, I still am. I had a fellow nerdy friend by the name George. Okay, he was just nerdier than me. But George was just brilliant.

We worked together on many science projects from CO2 lasers to plasma loudspeakers. The last time I saw George was years later in Houston, Texas where he was working on a device called an Uninterruptable Power Supply (UPS). Like I said, he was brilliant. Along with his brilliance he had a very pragmatic outlook on life, you could say he was a left-brain dominant person. He believed in nothing he could not prove with the scientific method. He could be described as rational. On two separate occasions I was about to rock his world and neither of us could have guessed what was about to happen.

We both had a great interest and enjoyed the fantastic music of the day. Remember, this was only two years after Woodstock. We had heard of a new Hi-Fi audio store and decided to go check it out. Also, rumor had it that there were some incredible loudspeakers they were selling. About a week after our UFO sighting on the river, we decided it was time to check the place out. We arrived and I led the way across the parking lot in my hippy jeans, boots, tie-dyed T shirt, and my huge belt buckle on all of 135 pounds of me. Not a care in the world. I opened the glass door and stepped in.

As I said, our world was about to be rocked forever.

I stepped in about six steps when a smallish man approached me. He was dressed entirely in black except for his starched, white shirt. He had curly black hair, dark complexion, and a ruddy face. Deeply pitted from acne perhaps.

He moved toward me in the most peculiar way. He did not approach me with a smile and a friendly handshake, oh no, he moved to within inches of my face in a blink of an eye. Black eyes inches from mine. A very accurate description would he moved like a Komodo dragon lizard lunging toward its prey. He stood before me, hunched over with his face looking slightly down not yet meeting my eyes. As he rose up, our eyes met, I felt THE most uncomfortable sensation, a cold vacuum sucking the heat out of the room, a sensation of terror. Then it hit me, an intense intrusion into my most private thoughts. I felt totally helpless. I was being mentally raped. I could not break away from his stare. Then it happened. As he finished probing my every thought, he grinned the most evil, terrifying grin one could imagine and said "HHHHHiiiiiiiiii" still moving in that reptilian way. As he rose to stare into my eyes, he thrust out his right hand to shake mine. He grinned and his lifeless, mocking eyes flashed a laser-like red from inside his pupils. I was beyond terrified. This was a level of fear probably felt by very few. This was the most intimidating person, "thing" I have ever met, then and now in 70 plus years. As he had his hand out something inside me screamed "don't touch him." If my heart had not been pounding so hard, I assuredly would have passed out. All of this took place in just seconds. I backed away refusing to shake his hand which he still extended toward me with that evil grin. I managed to back out the door and run to the car. George was already at the car. That was the fastest I had ever seen George move.

As we sat down in the car, we looked at each other, both terrified said "WTF was THAT." We were both shaking which, as we drove away, turned to very nervous laughter. George had seen the whole thing just a step behind me. He looked as terrified as I was. I know this "event" would forever change his perspective of the nature of reality; it certainly did mine. Thinking back, I believe it scared him more than me. As unprepared and shaken as I was, he had to have been even more so.

A few weeks later I got up the nerve to call the audio store to inquire about this "salesman." I was concerned about talking to the same man. Luckily, I was able to speak with the owner of the business. He was nice and accommodating. I asked him if he had employed a man that fit the physical description of the person/ "thing" that we had encountered at his store appearing as a salesman. "No sir, I have not, nor would I employ someone fitting your description of this person" he replied.

I have had many years of thoughts about this creature from our nightmares, and have come to some conclusions with the help of some others that have experienced similar events.

A) Luckily, I have not encountered such a being in a half century, and I hope I never again experience such an event. If I do, I would be more prepared. My conclusions on the possibilities of what this being is or was are: A Man in Black. Much unlike the lovable *Men in Black* (MIB) movie characters in the movies, these guys are said to be terrifying to the unlucky people who are approached by them. They usually approach someone if they have reported a UFO to authorities or have seen a UFO or had a close encounter of any degree. The MIB warn the person(s) not to talk about their encounter in any way under the penalty of death or some other terrifying misfortune. And most comply. It was exactly one week after our UFO sighting on the river.

B) Demonic entity. This possibility is terrifying. With all the other events in either the "real world" or the "dream world" happening to me I might have gotten someone's or something's attention. Speaking with more knowledgeable people about this over the years, the red eyes are a dead giveaway for demonic presence. I simply cannot easily convey how utterly terrifying this encounter was, not just for me but for George as well. This is much more horrifying than any movie I have since seen involving demonic entities and the characters in those movies.

C) A Reptilian humanoid. This is even more terrifying. If this was a reptilian, I can completely understand why other individuals encountering these beings were/are terrorized. If they can do what was done to me, they are a formidable foe and not to be tested.

D) Human. If this is true, and I am not convinced, this would be the strangest person on earth with some definite mental powers of mind control. He could have been trained to do so. He could be immortal. But he (it) was far from normal.

A few weeks after, I was sitting on the roof of my parent's house that stood high above a lock and dam on the Arkansas river. The same house I spoke of earlier that my friend witnessed the huge, cylindrical mothership. I had my Bolex Super 8 camera mentioned earlier. I noticed a very bright, white light to the north about 10 -15 miles away. It looked like a beam type light that was pointed east. As soon as I was aware of it, it turned to the south and pointed directly at me. I was startled by its swift turning direction toward me, also I felt as if I was noticed and that it was very aware of me. I felt very self-conscious for some reason! It was an odd feeling. There are some people today that claim to have experienced crafts responding to their thoughts. I deduced that whatever this object was, it responded to my being aware of it. Even at the distance it was from me it was bright enough to peg my light meter off scale high in my camera. That is incredibly bright. It changed direction again to the east and moved that way. I got down of the roof and called someone at Camp Robinson which was and is currently a military training facility which was about 15 miles to the north. They had no night training going on. No helicopters or planes. Something I forgot to mention. I did not have any film in my camera. I know, I know, I can hear it now. Why did you not have film in your camera? A valid question. Remember this was a film camera. It had limited exposure capabilities at night. Also, I did not have any film, so I was utilizing it as a monocular lens to see things at a distance.

The Philadelphia Experiment (Project Rainbow)

Real Event

Another odd event occurred that year. A few weeks earlier I met Bill, an older fellow who was a friend of Stan that he met at church. We all had interests in electronics. Stan was a friend that I knew from junior high school and had many adventures with.

On a Friday night Bill had a surprise, he wanted us to meet an old friend whom I will refer to as "The Man" that he knew from World War II. It has been too many years to remember his name. Stan and I went with Bill to meet him and we sat down for a chat. The Man offered us a beer and of course we partook gladly. The evening started off with interesting conversation. The current of that conversation took us down a river I had never taken before. The man asked us if we had ever heard of the "the Philadelphia Experiment." Of course, I had not and he proceeded to talk about what it was. (Most people have heard of it by now with the books and movies, however, I had heard about the Philadelphia Experiment fifteen years before the subject was popularized in the media. This now lends at least some credibility to The Man's claims.)

I never asked the man his age, which would be rude, but I estimated him to be in his fifties at that time of summer of 1971. That would put him around 20 to 30 years old in 1943.   For those who have not heard the incredible story here we go.

He started by saying he was involved as a civilian tech for some corporation unknown to me.

In 1943, at the peak of war cargo ships and Allied Fleets were being ravaged by German U-boats. The carnage was staggering. Someone in the Navy Intelligence had the idea to create a device that would render Allied Ships "invisible" to radar and underwater magnetic detection. The idea was posited that a strong electromagnetic field could generate a "bubble" around any ship that would give it "stealth" capabilities using today's vernacular, rendering any ship invisible to enemy radar. The man claimed the ship chosen for this experiment was an escort vessel named the USS Eldridge. The project was Code name "Rainbow." It is said by other sources later that both Einstein and Tesla were involved. Also, allegedly the group leader was John Von Neumann. Who would later be credited as the creator of modern computer software and helped in the development of the atomic bomb. The "Radar Invisibility" experiment was held in the Delaware River just removed from the Philadelphia shipyards. What was about to happen to the ship and her crew was totally unexpected and horrendous. Early on the morning of October 23, 1943, the experiment began. The generator spun up; the field coils were switched on. Nothing happened at first. After a few seconds the testing radar lost the blip on the screen of the Eldridge. Success! Cheers and applause went up from the onlookers. The Eldridge was now invisible to radar. Their hard work had paid off. In seconds a green mist formed around the ship. Seconds later the Eldridge and her crew simply vanished. What was supposed to be radar invisible was now invisible to the eyes of everyone watching. People reported seeing the outline of the hull displacing the water around it. A depression in the water in the shape of the hull. Then it was gone. The ship was no longer in the river.

Of course, there was total surprise then total panic. The Man claimed he witnessed the whole event from the test control facility in the shipyard. Approximately a minute later the USS Eldridge winked back to its original location.

The Man claimed the ship, on its return, did not look right, something had gone terribly wrong. It was smoking hot, parts of the ship were gone or moved to another location on the ship, there were crew members wandering the deck. All dazed, some were all right, some badly burned, some were still burning, many sailors jumped off the ship to escape the heat. But a few were fused into the deck and walls of the ship dying a horrible death. Of course, the entire event was covered up. Some people later were allegedly "suicided" to keep things quiet.

The Man had heard that the remaining Eldridge crew who survived were kept sequestered to control the rumors and to treat them. It is alleged by others that there were strange events among the surviving sailors such as some "Phasing" in and out, walking into walls and never returning and spontaneous human combustion. I asked The Man why he would reveal alleged top-secret material to some teenagers. His reply was "I am dying from cancer, and no one would believe teenage boys anyway." He was right, most people will still find it too fantastic to believe even today.

With my eighteenth year being a very active time in my life in many ways there were more events that set me on my current path of discovery. This strange conversation with The Man gently pushed me into a current of unsettling feelings that I could no longer trust what the federal government or any government could or would say about these types of research being carried out in the name of "national security" ever again. The so called "Philadelphia Experiment" was needed at the time to reduce losses of men and material on the Atlantic transports disrupted by German U-boats. Most involved believed it was worth the risks. When the test went terribly wrong it had to be covered up. It would have been an embarrassment. With low moral about the war at the time it was understandable to keep it quiet from the public almost to the extent of the Manhattan Project. However, when the war was over it should have been declassified but it was not, maybe for the reasons there may have been information from the experiment that was used for later experiments and were still considered classified.

Mother Ship

Real Event

At this time in my life, I was heavily involved in making amateur films on Super 8MM film. In those days there were no personal video cameras. I later purchased a Bolex 16MM camera, until now I only had a Bolex Super 8MM. I loved that camera.

It was beautifully constructed and operated flawlessly. Steve D., a good friend, asked me to film a movie he wanted to make called *The Packer Gang*. We got some friends together and shot it over a few weeks in the summer of 1971. It was a terrible film, but it had sound, dialogue, music, and special effects. It was a blast to make, and we all enjoyed making it. At my parent's house I had constructed a film editing room to add the sound and edit the films we made. Steve and I were up late one night editing the film. We got tired and Steve decided it was time to go, and he left the house around 3 a.m. After he walked out and closed the door, I went to the kitchen to get something to eat before I went to bed. He drove a Volkswagen Beetle. This car had a very distinct engine sound. It had a high-pitched chirp at each stroke of one of four pistons. As I was gulping down my cereal, I noticed he had not started the engine yet. I started toward the door when I heard him start it up and he drove away. The time from him walking out the door and starting his engine was at least 5 minutes. I thought this was odd. I was right, it was odd, very odd.

The phone rang about 7 a.m. and Steve was on the other end. He was totally freaked out; I do not think he got a wink of sleep that morning. Frantically he exclaimed that he had seen something right above my house at the time he left. Now I knew why he had delayed his departure. He said he watched it for about 5 minutes which matched my timeline. Since we had grown up together, we often played practical jokes on each other. So, I did not put that possibility aside. I asked him if he was joking with me and he was emphatic that he was not. So, I left it at that. Twenty-one years later at our class reunion in 1992 I asked him again the story that occurred that night. There was no hint of deception, and all the facts remained the same. Also, memory is not always accurate, so I had to ask him again and many years in between asking, the story stayed the same.

Note: If someone is lying especially over time the "facts" most often change or they do not remember or do not want to talk about it.

I wish now I could have seen the craft that night, I envy his experience. It must have been awe-inspiring.

He described it as a huge cylinder-shaped craft that was hovering over my house and made no sound. He described the ship as having rows of windows and lights along the hull. Search lights scanning the lock and dam just below my house. He said it was huge, at least as long as a football field. Next the search lights extinguished, and the craft just disappeared.

He was not "into" the subject matter of UFOs and had no previous knowledge of the different types of craft. It turns out his description was spot on accurate. I seriously doubt he could have known the configuration of such a craft, as there was little information available at the time. In those days, with very limited information and certainly no internet, even I was only somewhat knowledgeable about this type of craft. By today's description what he allegedly witnessed would be referred to today as a "Mother Ship," much like today's air craft carriers. Most probably used for interstellar and/or interdimensional travel. The thought of thousands of tons of metal, or whatever it was made of, hovering over my house is troubling. Whatever propulsion they are using is capable of lifting tons with the ease of lifting a feather in the breeze. Still, I envy his experience. Few people have seen such a craft, especially up so close even to this day. However, I have a strong feeling that we as a civilization will see many more in the coming years.

Grand Torino

Real Event

A few weeks later George and I had another adventure together, sort of. George asked me to go on vacation with him and his mother to go visit relatives in Ohio. I think he did not want to be alone on the trip with his mother. I accepted his offer and a few days before we were to leave, I got a very distinct "warning" not to go. I sensed there was danger. It was a feeling I find difficult to describe, maybe a constrained defined concern of some uncertain, impending doom. Today we would say that my "Spidey" senses were going off. After such a clear warning I simply could not go with them. Sadly, I informed George of my decision. He was very disappointed, and I could tell he simply could not understand my reasons. It hurt him and I was sad about it. After that day our friendship would never be the same again.

Four days later I got a call from George. He said they were back home. They were supposed to be on vacation for over a week. He asked me to come over. He lived close by, so I went to see what was wrong. There was a new car in the driveway. He came outside with an odd look, sort of an embarrassed grin on his face. He said, "Now I understand why" and explained why they got home so soon. It turned out they were passing through Cleveland and had picked up a hitch hiker. George was driving, his mother was riding shotgun, and the hiker was in the right rear seat. In that situation, I would have been sitting in the left rear seat. A drunk ran the red light, plowing into the left rear door. Their car, a red Grand Torino was totaled. I would have been badly injured or even killed. So, from that experience I learned to listen to these warnings for the rest of my life, sometimes to the dismay of others. I no longer drive red vehicles. I had thirteen accidents in red vehicles of various kinds in my life. I have fallen once or twice by not heeding the warnings and I have paid dearly for it.

George had a very "scientific mind," everything had to be proven to his satisfaction. When he returned early from his trip, he had a look of defeat and an acceptance that there was truly more to the world than science can prove at that time, or even now. You see, he simply could not understand how I could have possibly known that something terrible would happen if I went with him. It was simply incomprehensible to him. We ALL have this sense, this awareness but most of us ignore it or bury it deep inside because we fear it and from the programming, the reactions from our family and friends we receive nonstop from the world. A world programmed from birth to accept the world just as George did, only physical occurrences are real and provable.

Yes, the world has been pulled over our minds. A Matrix--system that keep society bound to traditional ways of thinking and living--or "womb" of disinformation designed to keep us at a low mental frequency that predominately insinuates that we are nothing, we must consume, reproduce, pay our taxes, and compete for swiftly diminishing natural resources. But, often, glitches do occur in the matrix. More, many more glitches will occur in the coming years. The veil of forgetfulness and awareness is falling.

That fall, George went on his way in life and I went mine. I did see him once in Houston, Texas years later when he was working on the UPS I mentioned earlier.

These types of events in my life now as I was getting older started to slow down and it may be years in between but they are still ongoing today.

TWENTY

It is That Simple

Real Event

In the remaining days of living with my parents and about to take my first scary steps out on my own I sat out on the warm concrete driveway of my parent's home in the summer night. I was apprehensive yet excited for the life to come on my own. At some point the chick must leave the nest to fly or not. On one special night I was asking the questions every human has asked since the beginning of the world.

I sat in lonely silence drinking in the warm summer night. I remember it very well. I asked the question, "what is the meaning of life, why are we here, what are we to do with the time we have been given?" The crickets fell quiet as a peaceful, loving presence, the likes you can only imagine, enveloped me, embraced me, and whispered in my right ear with the most beautiful voice I have ever heard on this planet. "To Be." The voice said as a whisper with calm and compassion. I could almost feel the breath in my ear. I sensed this being had a vast wisdom of all things in this world and beyond. Who or what spoke to me I do not know. It could be my guardian angel, Jesus or even God. I never saw anyone, just heard the voice. Whatever or whomever it was, it was a beautiful experience that I will never forget.

I had asked the questions that have probably been asked by every single person that ever lived and lives this day and ever will live. "What is the meaning of Life?" What is the meaning of life? The answer I was blessed with, that I am forever grateful for, was spoken with power, beauty, and love. The answer to my universal question was "To Be." A simple answer that defies the human mind that feels more comfort in the complexity of life. How could such an answer be so simple? I have found through the years the most profound answers are the simplest. Of course, we all have many flaws and one in particular stands out. That flaw is the tendency to divide and complicate even the simplest concepts, usually, to control the narrative, to seem brilliant in the eyes of others. The idea that life, in its simplest terms, is to just experience life. Good, bad, happy, or sad, complicated, or simple. We need not make it more complicated than it is but sadly we do.

Our purpose in life IS to BE exactly what we are. Whether you agree or not, we, all sentient beings, are immortal spiritual beings that inhabit human bodies to experience physical existence. Much like Jesus, we are here to experience the physical world, a world that is far too low of a frequency of energy for God to physically exist. God needs beings to experience the material world as proxies. Physical life is an experiment in free will. Life is the ultimate gift. So many are lost and take life for granted, they abuse and defile it, slapping the face of God for the gift of life, in defiance. It is time to understand that life is to experience life. Life IS a state of MIND. The universe is God's thought, maybe it is just his dream. All is mind!

What you sow, so shall you reap. The gift of free will, what can I say? A gift that even the Angels have not, a gift of freedom to choose your own destiny. That my readers, IS REAL POWER, THAT IS TRUE FREEDOM. It is not freedom from life; it is within life.

If you had a parent that gave you the most precious of gifts ever, would you slap them in the face for it? Be grateful for ALL you have and even more gifts will be given to you. Be grateful for even the worst of experiences for they all contain a lesson that is a gift you need to learn. Are not the best learned lessons the hardest learned lessons?

With all the comprehension I could muster, it was just too simple. You might be thinking "this was a more innocent time in his life" and you would be correct. But the message was to return to innocence, to a childlike wonder of life, to be whatever you choose. As I have grown older, those two words have grown as well. Grown in scope, complexity and... its simple message. This was a true gift of the loving spirit of ALL THAT IS, I am certain. I have seen that this simple statement ties disparate threads of my life together. It helped me to assemble pieces of life's vast puzzle into a more coherent vision. I lovingly implore you to burn those two words into your mind and heart for it is the key to life, a life with real meaning, a life without the shackles of guilt. It is a life of loving acceptance for what you are. Return to innocence of the spirit. This is what I learned.

A Real Event

Pay attention to ME!

On December 7th, 1973, my paternal grandfather died in his sleep in his Lazy boy chair. He passed on with ease and grace. You see, he had been a wonderful servant of God with his mission to bring alcoholics, ex-convicts, and broken men to God. On the day of his passing, he had been seen by his doctor and was pronounced fit. Maybe he was just ready to be in the presence of his Lord. I got the sad call from my mom to meet them at my grandfather's home to help comfort my grandmother. From the moment I walked in the door I felt an irritation of unknown origin that could be described as a tension on my left shoulder and up the side of my neck. I never felt it before, and I have never felt it since that day. It did not hurt but it was persistent. The coroner had removed grandfather's body earlier so all I could do was embrace my sweet grandmother in her great loss. I stayed for a while to make some leftovers for everyone while my parents tended to grandmother's needs.

I went home after that and watched some TV. Meanwhile, the irritation continued but had lessened somewhat. At about 10 p.m. I got a bedtime snack. Mom and Dad were still at my grandmother's house so I was all alone. I left the kitchen and went to the front door to check it for security, it was locked. A staircase faced the left side of the front door. As I made it about halfway up the stairs when the locked front door swung open hitting the wall and knocked a picture off the wall. It fell at the foot of the stairs. The door again swung and closed. I went back down the stairs and hesitantly checked the door; it was still locked. The irritation in my neck and shoulder was gone. The entire event took only seconds. It startled me at first, but I was not afraid, just spooked. I think I told my parents about it the next day.

I thought long and hard about what could have happened looking from my grandfather's point of view. This is only a theory.

He watched TV in his favorite chair and fell asleep. After he had slept, he woke up, got out of his chair, and heard his wife preparing their evening meal in the kitchen. He walked up to her and said something. She completely ignored him. He was puzzled with her lack of any response and was now a little irritated. He spoke to her again, and still no response. The irritation grew. Then he thought,

 is she going deaf? Is she playing with me? The irritation grew more combining with fear. He grabs her by the shoulders, to turn her toward his direction. She does not move, he grabs her again, still she does not move and ignores him still. He suddenly realizes his hands pass right through her body. A wave of fear passes through him. He tries again. He then becomes terrified and confused. What is happening to me? He rationalized and thought, "I'm still asleep and I'm dreaming, that's it." He goes back to his room with the chair and his TV. He sees an old man asleep in his chair. "What was going on, a stranger in my chair, how dare him, who is he?" He walked slowly up to the old man and looks carefully at him. He looked familiar somehow. The shock, the realization upon the very idea of it was too much. He cried out but no one heard it. He sat down on the floor for the first time in many years and cried, "I'm dead, how could this happen, the doctor said I was, OK?" My grandmother walked into the room to let him know his meal was ready and sees him sitting quietly in his chair. She realized something was wrong; she went to him and lovingly touched his hand. "Honey?" He was not breathing; his hand was cold. She called my dad to come over. Mom and dad came in the unlocked door; grandfather hears them and rushes to greet them. Again, he tried to get their attention with no results. He tried to talk with them and they do not see or hear him. He gets frustrated again. Then I walked in the door. The irritation, I believe, was a physical manifestation of grandfather trying desperately to get my attention maybe by poking me on the shoulder. I believe he rode home with me and followed me into my house. He continued in angry desperation to get my attention, and he had enough and when I started up the stairs to my bedroom, he opened the door behind me and walked out, slammed the door and he was gone.

Weeks later, I had a wonderful dream about seeing him for the last time. We sat on a grass covered hillside on a warm, sunny day somewhere in the Ozark Mountains. He had grown up in the Ozarks. We spoke of many things that sadly I do not remember but I do remember that he was happy.

When one is young, death is not a priority of thought. Youth believe they are immortal. As we grow older, we become more concerned and pre-occupied with death for we see the results with our grandparents, parents, and friends. The uncertainty of it all terrifies us, the pain, the cost, and the loss. As we arrive in the winter years the predator that stalks us starts to lose its teeth for those who believe in life after life. The sting of its bite becomes a love nip sometimes reminding us that everything is all right, the universe has our best interests in mind. Everything is recycled and whether we like it or not we are part of a grand cycle of life and death. Even the universe itself is recycled.

I am at the time of this writing 70 years on and just recently had a lesson in ACCEPTANCE. In my soul I kept hearing the word acceptance. It was a beautiful lesson of letting go of my resistance born out of the fear of the unknown. I have for a long-time feared death, not of fear of what lies beyond life but of the pain of death. Birth is just the opposite of death. A passing from the other side to this life accompanied by the pain of birth. The transition both ways can be painful. Our origins are from the other side so why do we believe it so terrible to go there? It is our true home. We fear the unknown so we must learn all we can about the truth of life and death to understand and lose our fear. More than ever, it is now possible to learn and understand.

TWENTY-ONE

Real Event

Hollow Men in the Dark

It was now 1974. My two brothers were both then employed as counselors at a state institution for young women who had brushes with the law. I visited them at the facility a few times and was apparently noticed by some of the young women there. Later I was invited to attend a party to help the girls unwind. This was a chance for them to understand how to have a fun time without the use of drugs and/or alcohol. The party wound down about 10 p.m. and I decided to head home. The night was humid and had started to cool off. I was now on a lonely stretch of road that had been an area where skirmishes occurred during the Civil War. A southern young man, David O. Dodd, had been caught and accused of treason and was hung by the Union troops in that area. I rounded a wide curve to the left and saw up ahead a fog bank crossing the road beneath tall towers that provided power to the area. In the fog I clearly saw two human-like forms crossing the road from my left. I slowed down to let them get all the way across. They moved slowly like they did not have a care in the world. They could not have been further than 50 yards away. I kind of giggled inside when I noticed one was tall and lanky; the other was short and round like the comedy team Mutt and Jeff. They were both in my sight for at least 15 seconds. As I got close to them, as I started to pass them on my right, I noticed something very strange. They were both hollow.

They both turned and looked at me as I passed them. Imagine the shape of humans taking up space in the fog but clear inside their form. As I passed them further, they disappeared into the fog that surrounded them completely. I got a very cold shiver down my spine. I looked in my rear-view mirror and saw nothing but the night. I said nothing to anyone about the incident until my oldest brother mentioned he had seen the same thing in the same place a few weeks after my experience, and I hinted at nothing as to keep suggestion by me to a minimum. I quizzed him about what he saw. He claimed what he saw was in a fog bank in the same area under the power lines, on the same road. He claimed he saw two men walking along the road at night, one was tall and the other short and round. When he passed them no one was there.

The problem was that they were invisible. There was a movie that came out many years after our experiences that showed a sequence in the film that an invisible man was only visible while he was surrounded by steam. Fog and steam are water vapor, right? Since his body displaced the steam cloud, he was a hollow man inside the steam. He was invisible but the steam showed his outline. This is exactly what I saw many years before the movie release, to my utter amazement. What were they? Ghosts? Possibly, I really do not know, all I know is that they were there and quite real. Some might argue that I had smoked a little too much weed and/or had a drink too many. Not so. The party was held for girls that were incarcerated at a state facility. No alcohol, no weed.

This road had been a battlefield during the Civil War so if you believe in ghosts, maybe that is what they were. There is another more disturbing possibility. I do not believe human invisibility technology was available in 1974, maybe now perhaps, besides, if it were two humans in cloaking technology why the hell would they be walking at night out on a lonely road? Not a very efficient use of exotic technology. It had occurred to me later in life that this technology could be a very useful tool for "Visitors" from elsewhere to observe humans without fear of ever being noticed by humans unless they cross a lonely road at night in a fog bank.

Addendum: A related story to the above, I had a good friend, Teddy, that passed from Covid-19 in 2021. He told me of an experience he had that had shaken him quite badly.

This was his story. One evening about ten years before his passing he was enjoying the summer dusk and a great cigar. There was still enough light to see well while he was looking down the road that led to his house. He noticed something creating a distortion in the air shaped like a man, on the road, moving toward him. It was clear but what he could see through it was shimmering. As it moved toward him, he became apprehensive. He was leaning against the left side of the bed of his truck. The shimmer did not break the shape's pace. Teddy's damaged heart was beating wildly now. This thing kept coming. He frantically looked for anything he could defend himself with. In the bed of the truck, he noticed a container of gasoline just slightly out of reach. As he lurched for the handle there was a flash of light. The next thing he knew he was lying on his bed with the same clothes on with the cigar still lit in his hand.

I for one think he had a brush with a real, unknown entity. It fits the description of what my brother and I had witnessed on that lonely road. I think it would be a safe bet that many have seen things like this.

It also fits the description of an entity that a famous UAP investigator's wife had while she was hunting alone in the woods near her house. Her description was that it was clear and it shimmered. It was sitting in a tree, not too far from her while she was in her deer stand. Simultaneously, there was a multi-witness UAP sighting at a school less than a mile away.

TWENTY-FIVE

Real Event

Close Encounter with Harry

In the year 1978, I decided I needed to visit a friend in Colorado. Keith B., the same Keith I had the meshing dream with mentioned earlier, had moved to Denver the previous year to work for a title company. His older brother had already moved out there and was engaged to be married soon. Bruce, Keith's brother asked me to bring his fiancée to him in Denver. I obliged and we set out for Denver. We had an eventful trip stopping and camping next to Lake Meredith in the Texas panhandle. A storm came up that night and we experienced lightning and high winds. I had never experienced a storm in the desert and had not ever thought a desert storm could be so wet. We woke up the next morning to about 2 inches of very slick mud surrounding my car. Thank goodness we were camping in the car. I had no camping equipment including a tent. The only way out was to climb a hill that had been soaked that night and of course covered in mud. I could not get any traction at all. I was getting worried that we could not get out and I had to think out of the box. What could I do? Since I had a front wheel drive car maybe putting the car in reverse and backing up the hill would do it. YES, IT WORKED! What a relief! We got out of there and headed northwest to Denver. It took us a while to find Keith and Bruce's apartment. In those days there were no cell phones, and no apps, only maps. Keith had arranged ahead to take two days off from work so we could go camping in the mountains and to let the two lovers get re-acquainted. Keith and I had been friends since our sophomore year in high school. He had decided to strike out and head west and ended up in Denver living for a short while with his older brother Bruce. After our camping trip he moved to Aspen for a while and then back home to stay. While he was in Aspen, he got to know some actors and other famous movers and shakers. One was named Jack, a well-known actor whom he liked to drink Jack Daniels with at a local bar.

We were very excited to be going up in the Rockies for a wild adventure and we got it. It was really my adventure, you see Keith was there, but he slept through the incredible part of the event. If you have never been to the Rockies please put them on your bucket list. They are absolutely beautiful, awe-inspiring and an important piece of our country's colorful history and culture. Keith and I packed our gear and took off for them thar hills. We decided to stop and get two Styrofoam ice chests, buy groceries and ice, and continued west on Interstate 70. We climbed ever upward the eastern slope toward the

Eisenhower Tunnel. A while before we entered the tunnel, we lit up a joint and got higher than the mountains that surrounded us. We entered the mouth of the beast and I felt like we were falling into the abyss all the while listening to Alan Parsons *I Robot*. It reminded me of the wormhole that Commander Bowman went through in the movie *2001 A Space Odyssey*.

The tunnel is over a mile long and is one of the highest in the world, also, it bores through and under the Continental Divide which on the eastern slope America's rivers flow east and the western side all the rivers flow toward the west. This area of Colorado is the birthplace of many rivers, the Arkansas, the Blue, Platte, of course the Colorado, Rio Grande, and more. As we started down the western slope, following the Colorado River, we turned off to the left and headed south toward Leadville.

Leadville is a small mountain village that is just a pass-through kind of place not far from South Park, and it had a rich past.

The last shootout that Doc Holiday had was in a saloon in Leadville with a disgruntled poker player. He had enough of life at this point and headed east to say goodbye to Wyatt Earp at the Windsor Hotel in Denver. He ended up in Glenwood Springs, dying alone in a sanitarium from consumption, passing into history.

Leadville is just downstream from the headwaters of the Arkansas River. There, the river is a beautiful trout stream formed from melting snow higher up. And lastly, Leadville is most famous for being a very successful mining town. The surrounding mountains held the mines owned by the famous "unsinkable" Molly Brown, and her husband. She was a very lucky woman because she was one of the few who survived the sinking of the Titanic.

The first night we camped on a creek just between Twin Lakes and Aspen. That night we had steaks and beer. It was a special time. We slowly move up to Independence Pass the next day, spent a long time on the mountain tops. We went down the western side and arrived in Aspen. We had lunch, explored the town, and bought some more food. We then headed west to see the Maroon Bells. If you have never been, go see them, they are breathtaking. Two mountains shaped like giant bells pushed into the ground and rise thousands of feet above your head and the rock that makes them are various shades of Maroon and a clear lake reflecting the mountain's majesty. As the day moved on, we decided to check out the Aspen Highlands, another mountain valley just to the east of the Maroon Bells. It was getting late, we picked a spot just off the main road and lit up a warm fire, drank a beer, had dinner, and relaxed. There was a cold trout stream nearby that kept us company. It was a few feet away and I took the coldest bath I have ever had before or since. When you are in a mountain valley the sun goes down over the west mountain, the afterglow lasts for a few hours and the opposite happens in the morning. My car was a Volkswagen Sirocco, a sportier version of the popular Volkswagen Rabbit. It had the ability to remove the back seat and position it against the two front seats to form a nice bed for two people. It beat the heck out of setting up a tent and this particular evening it would be our protection as well.

We slept well that night after we had placed the two Styrofoam ice chests on top of the car. We did not want to wake up the next morning to find food strewn all over the campsite.

About six a.m., with the forementioned morning glow in the air, I awoke to the distinctive squeak of Styrofoam being pulled across the top of the car. Someone was trying to steal our food. OH SHIT! I had a hickory axe handle with me for such possible situations. I tried to wake Keith as quietly as I could so I would have reinforcements. He just snored. On my side of the car something was pressing up against the window. I felt the car move from the shifting of something's mass. I carefully wiped the condensation from the driver's side window. I saw fur! OH SHIT, SHIT! It was about 3 inches long. It had black, and brown mixed together. The only thing I could see of this thing was its waist with the fur up against the window. This had to be a brown bear or worse a grizzly. I realized my hand was no more than a quarter of an inch from its body with only the glass between us. My mind was working fast thinking what were my options. Since I had the car between me and whatever it was, I decided to yell "Who's there?" It kind of popped out. The "bear" froze. It hesitated and stopped pulling on the ice chest. It released the ice chest, then it quietly backed away a few inches leaving the ice chests and I still could not make out what it was yet. It was probably confused by my screaming voice coming out of this red, metal thing. It made no aggressive move, no sound so I waited a few seconds grabbed my axe handle and did the stupidest thing I have ever done.

I grabbed the door handle with my left hand and opened the driver side door, pushing against the "bear" and yelling at the top of my lungs. I got out screaming like a crazy man, waking

Keith up. NOW he wakes up, and in the twilight about twenty feet away was what I thought was a giant man in a thick furry coat running into the brush. Flushed with adrenalin, still screaming at Keith to get up, I realized this was no bear, it ran fast on two massive legs and was a least eight feet tall. This was a bipedal creature. I had eyes on it for about 5 seconds before it flowed into the trees. So, what the hell was it? I have seen many times since this encounter, bears recorded getting into food containers, tents, and backpacks. One two separate occasions I have been in the presence of two black bears. The bears always appeared clumsy, throwing things about in a chaotic fashion. This creature was very stealthy, very precise in its movements trying to get our food. This is why I thought it was a human trying to rob us.

Years later, after the movie *King Kong* by Peter Jackson was shown in theaters around the world with great success, the Public Broadcasting System (PBS) presented a Special on "The Real King Kong."[3] The documentary presented evidence of a prehistoric ape known as Gigantopithecus. Evidence showed that this giant ape species inhabited Asia and possibly the Americas 30 to 40 thousand years ago and allegedly went extinct at the beginning of the Younger Dryas period, around 12 thousand years ago. Most species were wiped out maybe not all. They most likely came across the ice bridge connecting Siberia and Alaska. I cannot say whether the species did or did not go extinct but is it not possible the Gigantopithecus is the ancestor to modern-day Sasquatch? Anthropologists are finding today and

---

[3] https://pbs.org (2024), Monstrum series.

have found living species that allegedly were believed to be extinct such as the famous Coelacanth. Life can be amazingly resilient.

As I was watching the PBS special with great interest, about 45 minutes in the narrators began a brief history of sightings around the country. It was pretty much the same history we have all heard about. Then it got very interesting. They got into the history of sightings in Colorado. I instantly perked up. Not anywhere else, just Colorado. Anthropologists had done a study of sightings relating to the locations at certain times of the year such as seasonal migrations to certain suspected feeding areas. When they displayed a map of the routes/sightings and guess where they converged? You got it! The ASPEN HIGHLANDS. Exactly where Keith and I camped that fateful evening.

Was it a Sasquatch? Do they really exist? After all the crazy, odd things I have experienced can I not ask that question? For me the answer is yes, you see, humans have discovered many other Simian (Ape) species all over the globe even "Hobbits." Not like in the movies about hobbits but a small ape-like creature. Of course, I am not the only person to come across a Sasquatch. Many sightings have occurred all over the planet. A question, if you lived in the vast reaches of forests in the world and all you had known were the trees and the animals of the forest and you came across a human or a group of humans acting loud, yelling, laughing burning fires and sleeping in weird, colorful things would you not hide and watch in wonderment at the weird crazy creatures draped in colorful strange garments invading your territory? A giant, hairy, intelligent creature that is shy already is well known: gorillas. Is it really such a stretch that another ape species could exist alongside us? Why is there no evidence for their existence? Maybe there is such evidence we just have not found it yet or if found, hidden away. In my research for this document, I have found many instances of our past being systematically removed, denied, and obfuscated by the scientific establishment and the governments of this world. I believe there is an ongoing effort to hide our true history on this planet. Why you might ask. "The powers that be" are afraid we might discover something that will shake the very foundation of our civilization. It would threaten their control of the narrative.

Even though humans dominate the world we have not explored on foot vast regions of forests many times greater than the urban and rural areas we live in. Yes, we have vast road systems but they cover only a tiny fraction of area of land. Unless we would stay in these vast, wild areas for years we could easily miss them. Why are there no remains? If they are intelligent, family oriented, very social among themselves they probably are extremely human-like. I would think they might bury their dead just as we do. These creatures are at least as intelligent as we are and they know we would be looking for their remains. They know the terrain down to the twig where they live. Lastly, we hunt them with guns. If I were one of them, I would get as far away from humans as I possibly could. Maybe if we approach them peacefully with respect, they might just reveal themselves. The way humans are so disrespectful of nature today I would hide as well.

I want to let you in on a little secret. Just because someone is educated in a flawed education system does not mean they are always correct or an expert. We are often bedazzled by scientific claims and scientific theories. If one is taught what to think, not How to think, is wrong (garbage) then the result of that person's thinking is garbage. One cannot ever make correct (proper) decisions with erroneous information. That not only goes for individuals but for a society, even an entire civilization. I will cover this topic again in Part Two.

For many years afterward I could not wrap my head around the idea I had encountered one. One other thing that I did not think of until recently. I just may be the only person currently to get within a quarter of an inch from one. My hand was only the thickness of the glass away from its body. I watch shows on television and have never seen or heard of anyone getting that close. I feel so blessed to have experienced this creature and I am very glad I am still alive to tell you this true story!

TWENTY-SIX

Real Event and a Serial Dreams/Memories

Two Iron Ships and a Girl

At this point in my life, as I was now an adult with adult issues, I started to feel more pressure to get my life on track. I was, at the time, an audio design contractor. I was making a living somewhat but by no means getting rich.

A few years before this time in my life, I started having dreams or memories about being a soldier in the Civil War. The dreams/memories manifested as what I call "serial dreams." They showed me a detailed, coherent story in succession and they lasted about a year. As you will soon see, I was not the only person to experience this phenomenon.

The first dream starts on a very rainy night. I remember marching, endless marching somewhere toward a worse situation. I was tired, hungry, wet, and scared. I was in rags. As we approached our destination I saw and heard activity around a ship. I made it out to be a steam driven river boat apparently to take us to a prison camp no doubt. As we approached the gangplank someone started shouting ahead of me, there was a struggle and shots fired. In the confusion I saw a chance to escape. I ran toward the cold, dark river as fast as I could. There were others doing the same thing I was doing, running, which increased my chances of getting away free. I remember shots and the sound of angry bees flying past me. A soldier to my left got hit and I could immediately smell that iron smell, a red mist in the air, the smell of a life extinguished forever. If you have never been shot at, the sound of a bullet is like an angry fast flying bee or hornet if you are unlucky and lucky to hear it and live. It is a sound you never forget. I know this because I have been shot at in this life.

The shocking cold of the water energized me to swim, swim for my life. I was escaping, swimming down river with the current to where, I had no idea, I did not care.

There were other minor dream/visions that are muddled and/or mundane to mention here but they were still part of the sequence. Through the months of these serial dreams I came to realize that I was a Confederate soldier and there were hints that I was an officer, possibly a Lieutenant.

The next important dream/vision was I remember staying in the river for quite a while to evade the soldiers that were hunting me. Dogs would be mostly useless while being in fast moving water or so I thought. As I floated down the river for days, starving and tired, one morning I awoke to the sound of heavy cannon fire in a bay that spread out below my position. This cannon fire was different however. When a shot was fired there was a sharp ping of metal being hit hard as if it would crack. As I moved further down into the bay the light got brighter and I could see better what was happening. I was shocked to see two very odd (ships)? Blasting each other at close range, the shells would bounce off with that loud metal ping. These ships were not what I was used to seeing at all, they were something new, something revolutionary. Even at close range they could not inflict significant damage to each other. Afterwards, for what seemed like a few of hours of blasting each other, the engagement ended. The smaller one drove off the larger one, protecting the Union wooden ships nearby.

I was intrigued by this battle and I found out in a history class that this was a battle that took place between the USS Monitor which was a Union ship and the CSS Virginia a Confederate ship. The Virginia was made from the sunken Union Ship, the USS Merrimack. The Merrimack was burned and scuttled as allowing the ship never to be used again but the lower hull survived and was salvaged by the Confederates and covered on the top with iron clad to deflect bombardment. It was slow and unwieldy. Its main weapon, however, was a battering ram to impale the wooden hulls of the Union blockade ships which proved effective until it broke off early in the battle. The Monitor, a northern ship, was very odd in its design that was more iron than iron cladding. It sat very low in the water to be less of a target, and it had a cylindrical turret with two heavy cannons mounted inside the turret on top of a flat deck. It was called "a cheese block on a raft." It was a radical design that "launched "pun intended, a new breed of war vessels, Iron ships, and the beginning of the end of sailing, wooden war vessels. The battle took place on the morning of March 8th, 1862. It began about 8 a.m. and both ships withdrew about noon, each believing they had won. It is now considered a draw.

The last dream/vision I had was to be an impossible synchronicity. I still, to this day, think what was meant to happen was for a reason, to teach me a valuable life and spiritual lesson. It starts out on a beautiful spring morning. I had stayed close to the river for some time to find food and to hide when I had to. To my left was the river, to my right, toward the south was a sown field and in front was a wooden bridge over a creek flowing into the river. As I was walking down the dirt road, I heard horses coming up fast from behind. Union soldiers were hot on my trail. I must have done something careless to alert them of my presence. I remember turning to my right to run diagonally to a small stand of trees on my side of the creek bank. Running across the field, I was almost to the trees when something hit me in the back so hard it threw me to the ground. Then I heard the report, too late, I had been shot in the back. The bullet burned into me and hit me like a sledgehammer blow. The impact was in my right kidney area close but not hitting my spine just below my lowest rib. I must have gone numb and passed out for a moment. The soldiers came up to me to see if I was dead. I was semi-awake but could feel no pain. I must have been in shock. One of the soldiers kicked me in the wound to see if I would make a sound. It took the last bit of strength not to. They cursed me, spat on me, and left me for dead. I must have passed out again for a while because it was late in the day and it was getting cold. I remember lying on my painful back looking up at a sycamore tree. I was terribly cold now. Since I could not move, I had the idea to cover myself with the huge leaves to maybe get warmer. I blacked out again.

Remember Steve D., the friend I made the film with? In 1979 he had moved away and left a beautiful girlfriend behind to go seek his fortune and fame. Enter Sherry. She was a sweet, pretty, blonde. A wonderful girl. I had known her through her relationship with Steve. One day she came over to my apartment just to get acquainted. We did and she asked me to dinner at her apartment. We had a wonderful dinner, drank some wine, and talked for a long time. The conversation turned to weird dreams that we giggled over. We were having fun with the whole idea, she felt relaxed and started to tell me of a "series" of dreams she had growing up that had left a strong impression on her.

It began with a walk to the riverside with a young slave girl who was her friend and playmate. The impression I got was that they were in their teens. They were walking along a creek that flowed into the river nearby. She told me they lived on a plantation. The plantation had to be in Virginia on the James River. The battle of the ironclads took place in the river merging into the Chesapeake Bay off Hampton Roads.

My interest perked up at this point, and understand I have said nothing about my dream/visions to Sherry. She continued, the cotton seed had not been sowed yet for it was still too cold. There were large trees towering above their heads. At this point I asked her what kind of trees they were. She thought a moment, "The trees had large leaves, cottonwoods or sycamores" I think. I almost blurted out in surprise, but I held it back and remained silent.

 She continued, as they walked along the creek both heard a groan nearby. They were scared at first then realized there was no threat. They approached where the groan was coming from and saw clothing under the fallen leaves that were covering a man that was barely alive. Sherry uncovered the man to get a better look. He was a southern soldier. "YOU were wounded, YOU had been shot," she exclaimed, and I was startled yet I kept my composer and calmly asked where the soldier had been shot. Sherry swung her right hand to her back and showed me. "You had been shot in the right side of your back just below the ribs," she explained. I was floored! She sent her slave friend to get someone with a cart as she stayed with the soldier. "We took you to the plantation so we could nurse you back to health." She had said "YOU" instead of him five times all the while not realizing it.

I was of course, astonished! After she told me her story, I brought it to her attention and she was perplexed, she had no idea what she had said or why. Hold on, it gets better.

She continued with her story. She brought the soldier back home, had "him" placed in a guest bedroom. Sherry remembered nursing "me" back to health and as time went on, she came to love him. After a few weeks he had begun to get better, enough that he was healthy and walking around. One day he decided he needed to go back to the war because the news of the war was going badly for the South at that point in time. He had been away far too long. According to Sherry they had grown close, and she was heartbroken that he was leaving her. The next morning, they said their goodbyes and he walked away, off to war. A few sad days went by when her father entered the front door, frantic, he said Union soldiers were coming. Her father told her to go upstairs with her slave girl companion and hide. They rushed upstairs and hid in a wardrobe. She heard the front door being beaten on. Someone answered the door, opened it and there was arguing between her father and the soldiers, there were shots fired. She thought her father had been killed and there were soldiers in the house looking for something, Sherry thought maybe they were looking for the soldier she had helped. The next thing she remembers was more shouting, then it became quiet. She smelled smoke, heard a fire, she was terrified but it was too late. Sherry said the last thing in her dream was the two of them, her and her friend died in the fire.

The crazy part that just blew me away was that she said "YOU" instead of "him." In my head I see this is a connection in these lives now that we live with those lives in the past. Reincarnation must be the reason for this situation. Until this happened, I was like you, that reincarnation was just a fancy idea, a dream to make us feel safer and more secure in this life.

ONE: I had serial dream/visions about being a Civil War prisoner, a southern soldier, Sherry had dream/visions of living in the South during the Civil War apparently on a plantation.

TWO: My dream/visions ended right where hers began.

THREE: Sherry referred to the soldier as "YOU" instead of "HIM" repeatedly.

FOUR: I had been shot in exactly the place Sherry described her soldier being shot.

FIVE: The chance of us meeting again to share those dream/visions is unquestionably impossible unless there is a mechanism in place to have people play out relational problems and issues from one life to the next. A life plan perhaps?

SIX: The real possibility that she loved me in that life as well as this one.

Referring to the beginning of this strange love story, the lesson I learned the hard way, which is often the most effective way to learn, that Sherry loved me and quite possibly loved me in other lives and in the two different lives I walked away from a love I could have had in both lives and possibly more.

As we all learn eventually, one way or another, love is the ONLY important thing in this and every world. I did not give Sherry the chance to love me or me to love her in return. To this day this is a painful lesson. Hindsight is 20/20 and I realized too late that I had messed up. Before this dinner discussion, I only imagined reincarnation as a wonderful idea but after that fateful dinner date that all changed for me. Is it so fantastic of an idea? An idea that dates back thousands of years. Did you know that even Jesus made a hint at its possibility? How could that be? Does reincarnation conflict with Christianity or any other religion for that matter? If you really think about it you should come to the same conclusion I did. There is no conflict. In the Book of Mathew, it is said that Peter, James, and John accompanied Jesus to a mountainside.

Matthew Chapter 17
[1] And after six days Jesus taketh Peter, James, and John his brother, and bringeth them up into an high mountain apart,
[2] And was transfigured before them: and his face did shine as the sun, and his raiment was white as the light.
[3] And, behold, there appeared unto them Moses and Elias talking with him.
[4] Then answered Peter, and said unto Jesus, Lord, it is good for us to be here:

if thou wilt, let us make here three tabernacles; one for thee, and one for Moses, and one for Elias.

⁵ While he yet spake, behold, a bright cloud overshadowed them: and behold a voice out of the cloud, which said, This is my beloved Son, in whom I am well pleased; hear ye him.

⁶ And when the disciples heard *it*, they fell on their face, and were sore afraid.

⁷ And Jesus came and touched them, and said, Arise, and be not afraid.

⁸ And when they had lifted up their eyes, they saw no man, save Jesus only.

⁹ And as they came down from the mountain, Jesus charged them, saying, Tell the vision to no man, until the Son of man be risen again from the dead.

¹⁰ **And his disciples asked him, saying, Why then say the scribes that Elias must first come?**

¹¹ **And Jesus answered and said unto them, Elias truly shall first come, and restore all things.**

¹² But I say unto you, That Elias is come already, and they knew him not, but have done unto him whatsoever they listed. Likewise shall also the Son of man suffer of them. ¹³ Then the disciples understood that he Spake unto them of John the Baptist.

"How could this be?" Jesus explained to them that Elias had returned in his cousin John the Baptist. How could Elias and John the Baptist be one? Elias was reincarnated as John to fulfill the prophecy.

OBE

The Golden City

I died again! I know, I know, it is crazy but it is true. When I was twenty-seven, I drove a truck, delivering air freight. It was in mid-November, I was on a delivery to Clarksville, about a hundred miles away from where I live when I became very sick. I drove that huge truck all the way home with the certainty I was dying. I was scared. It was during the influenza B epidemic of 1979-80 and it was epic. Many thousands died that year including me! You see I had a fever of a hundred and five. My doctor had prescribed Percodan to bring my fever down plus an antibiotic. It worked a little, but the combination of all the above effects took me over and beyond the edge.

What I will now reveal I considered for a long time to be a dream, a fantasy, a Percodan induced hallucination but became an event that began a long period of learning information about things beyond the physical world. It all happened for a reason. The reason is to teach us something important to our spiritual development. An Out-of-Body-Experience OBE that turned out to be shared by another person years later. Her shared truth was a confirmation of my experience. It was beautiful! "All That Is" had given me confirmation of life after so called "death." My fear of death has diminished. Not completely gone, the fear of the unknown is a powerful force. A fear of loss of the Ego, our individuality, snuffed out for eternity, yet not entirely. I discovered that what we experience in our different lives is downloaded to the Akashic Records[4] upon our death so that the collective may learn from our experiences as well. God seeks understanding of human life, we are its companions. Yeshua (Jesus),

---

[4] https//www.gaia.com (2025) What are the Akashic Records and What Are They For?

became human to experience life and to teach us his way, his path.

In this death experience I woke up in a bed that was not the bed I was sick in at my parent's house. At that moment I remember feeling more alive than even now. A blanket of golden, soft cloth covered the bed I was now laying in. It was a dark wood, four post type of bed with a shimmering golden shear cloth that was incredibly beautiful covering the top and all the sides.

It had the appearance of a delicate, golden hued rainbow. I gently brushed it aside, feeling that it might tear with the merest of my touch and got out of the bed. The floor was a very smooth stone like polished marble but not cold to the touch. The walls looked like adobe, like molded stone with curved corners. There was an open window to my left. I went to the window and looked out. I was up about twenty feet high. What I saw was shocking and wonderful. At the sight I now beheld I felt wonder, awe, and a glee that I cannot describe. I was overlooking a street of cobblestones of a golden color. Surrounding me were adobe style buildings for as far as my eyes could see to the horizon. The sky was the clearest dark blue violet imaginable. The star above me was not the sun that earth circles. This star was much larger and strikingly blue-white. The clouds were so bright white they were hard to look at directly. Off in the distance were snow-capped mountains surrounded by clean, clear air. I saw people going about their lives, busy in the street below. They all seemed happy. Then I heard a sweet voice call my name, "Good morning, Stephen," said a pretty woman dressed in a simple white robe flowing about. I do not remember who she was but apparently, she knew me. I was shocked to see that she was floating in the air at the second floor, same height I was. I think she giggled. WHAT? Where was I? Wherever it was, I knew this place somehow. I also knew I was back in the bed at home, sick still, but oddly I did not care, I was happy, truly happy. My body was heavy and still wracked with pain but I did not care. Somehow, I surged back to life and started to breathe painfully again, I was back. My lady friend at the time, Anita, was with me and said that I had been extremely quiet for a few moments.

A few years later, I do not recall the exact year, sometime in the mid-nineties, I was watching a documentary by a respected journalist on a broadcast channel. The documentary was focused on healing sciences and traditional medicine from around the world. Toward the end of the program, he was visiting a hospice house for terminally ill cancer patients in California. He sat in with a small group of women and asked them about what they were going through in their last days on earth. They all had a turn speaking of their peace or fears. Then a very special thing happened, an incredible thing. A woman who awaited her turn spoke up with a face expressing great peace in her acceptance of the end. She proceeded with, "I had a most beautiful dream last night and I just have to share it." For some unknown reason I was instantly alert to what she was about to say. In perfect synchronicity we both spoke the words together, "I woke up in a golden bed." As we spoke the words I was flooded with emotion and burst into tears of joy. I have no idea where that came from. Her story was very much like mine. To my utter amazement she described what I had experienced. It was beautiful! "All That Is" had given me confirmation of life after so called "death." My fear of death has diminished. I knew from that wonderful moment that a place is set for us. Whether it is Heaven or not I honestly do not know for certain, but it did feel wonderful and I was happy there, it felt like home. I am convinced that I was meant to see this program even if it was years later. So, I ask you, why should we be afraid of going back to our real home?

The Machine

A Powerful Download

What is a "Download Dream" you might ask? A download is a data dump of information of all kinds of subjects in a dream to prepare individuals for leadership and teacher rolls to instruct many thousands the ways of life that will replace the current life modalities when the current models fail. A "download" can come in many ways. Some have visions, some, automatic writing, channeling, etc. I my case they come in dreams of extraordinary detail that I remember most of, however, some information is "locked" to be opened at a pre-determined time for pre-determined purposes. This document may very well such information. On the 19th of November of 1979 when I was twenty-six, I received a "Download Dream", one of many. It was the kind of dream that you remember VERY well. It was a data dump concerning what I now call "The Machine." Many people all over the globe are now receiving these downloads now in preparation for something very important to the entire human race. No more secrets held out of reach from the common man. Ways of producing more energy than all of mankind could ever want to use, growing healthy food for all the world, extension of healthy lives, people living free of fear and violence. We will become a Type 1 civilization: a civilization that lives in spiritual and technical harmony with each other and the planet. Travel and trade with peoples of other worlds.

This dream download was an extremely powerful vision of machine-like diagrams, flow charts, and 3D images that flowed and moved like today's 3D computer graphics. It was so intense it overwhelmed me, but I do remember The Machine. I was instructed that if someone used it, they had to be perfectly trained and disciplined, their energy centers called chakras had to be perfectly aligned otherwise it would kill them, like spontaneous human combustion could do.

The device increases the electrical energy in the spinal column. The more energy flows the more open and coherent the spinal column must be with no electrical resistance to allow more energy to flow, safely. More about chakras later. Unfortunately, I cannot reveal the design for the warning I was given, it is simply too dangerous to the user, possibly too dangerous for everyone. Understand, I have a degree in Electronics Design and Implementation. Interestingly, this download is what motivated me to attain that degree. To continue with the honesty of the rest of this document I have to say that this machine quite possibly does nothing, just a dream, a very informative and powerful dream nonetheless, or it could be just the most powerful and or dangerous device ever conceived. For this reason, I have never built it. I feel strongly that the motive of the

Supervisor of the download had benevolent intentions. It may have been a test to see what I would do with it. In the end I still believe that the evolution of the human species needs to be a natural progression. We are in enough turmoil now as a species as it is. Adding this technology to the convoluted mess most likely would result in disaster. We are simply not mature enough to handle or even ready for this level of power.

As mentioned earlier the Supervisor may again have been Thoth. In the Emerald Tablets[5] allegedly written by Thoth, claims he was the designer and builder of the Great Pyramid. This would be a confirmation that the Great Pyramid is the first pyramid constructed over eleven thousand years ago. I have maintained this

---

[5] Https://gaia.com (2020) Emerald Tablet 101: The Birth of Alchemy

premise for many years. We have no reference to date the actual age of the pyramid's construction. Scientists can tell when granite was created but not when it was formed into a block. It was the template for later structures that simply could not be reproduced at the level of precision as the Great Pyramid. This is why the other pyramids have crumbled away. Much more about this in Part Two.

TWENTY-EIGHT

Real Event

The Séance and a Ouija Board

The year was 1981, I was now twenty-eight. I was invited to a séance at Dane's house. He was a good friend and schoolmate. It was a pleasant evening with drinks and conversation about spiritual things. Dane's mother asked if we would like to have a séance. We all agreed. After we all talked, we moved to the chairs around the dining room table. Someone had placed a large candle in the middle. We all put our hands on the table with the tips of our pinky's touching each other's pinky. A few moments went by in quiet meditation. Dane, sat to my right with his left pinky touching mine. Then something started to happen. I had my eyes closed going along with the plan. After a few moments I opened my eyes to see what was happening when I heard and felt Dane's left hand moving. Dane's left index finger started tapping. I heard a loud pop like someone popping their knuckles. Dane's finger rose even higher. He never took his hand off the table. I asked him if he was in pain, "No, I'm ok." It was tapping out a code or something I could not recognize. It kept on tapping, getting higher each time. I remember distinctly with his hand flat on the table, his finger was now 90 degrees straight up. With his hand flat the finger now was pointing backwards toward the back of his hand. Each time further it went back. I asked him again "Are you ok?" He said "It feels weird but it doesn't hurt." I do not know of any human that is capable of this hand movement especially with the palm flat on a table. This was not possible without damage to his hand. It kept popping, further it went until the tip of his finger almost touched the back of his hand. At that point I broke the circle. This was just too messed up. We did not continue with the séance after that. Everyone was too spooked.

I was so freaked out after the séance that a few weeks later I decided to remove and burn some reading material that I had purchased months before. Included was a Ouija board that my mom had given me for

Christmas years before. I built a blazing fire in the back yard that I was burning off some trash and decided to throw the books and the Ouija board on top. The books burned with no problems; however, the board was a very different matter. It would not burn! The fire was raging hot with all the books burning but that board just sat there. The paper that had all the print was singed off but for at least twenty minutes, the Ouija board-- nothing. At that point it finally caught fire but with an abnormal flame. It started hissing and blue flames shot out in different directions. They were like blowtorches, about six inches long. In an instant it went up in roaring flames and was gone. The Ouija board was made from Masonite, a hard brown paper board material that under normal circumstances would burn evenly and quickly because of the resins binding the board together. Not this time. I was glad to be rid of it. The house I was living in at the time was a rental that had a dark vibe about it. Strange things went on in that house. I was told that drug dealers lived there before me. I heard voices sometimes, had a furnace fire in the middle of the night, had break-ins and bad people around me. Not long after the Ouija board was destroyed my life started to get better. Not conclusive but interesting. Do each tie together? Unknown, but highly synchronized.

Some advice for the innocent. If you have a Ouija board, the ones that you have seen in various movies, please destroy them. Burn them if you can. Do not give them away! Do not leave them in your house. Of course, do not use them. I, like you, thought they were harmless. They are a manifestation of a portal. A two-way portal that is open to anything. The board is nothing on its own. It opens a portal within the user(s). That is the danger.

Think of them as telephones to the dead. Of course, you may get your grandfather or your mom but how would you know if it is really them? You could ask them a question that only they would know the answer? Well, you could but it does not work quite that way. You see, all entities, all souls, good or bad have access to a Universal Wide Web, or what is commonly called the Akashic Records. Every atom in this universe is connected and is information. A vast store of information recorded by every living soul about everything they have ever done that has ever lived or will ever live. It can be accessed by anyone at any time with the right training and awareness.

Knowing this would you trust just any site on the internet with all sorts of evil entities just waiting to snare you in their web of lies and danger? It happens all the time. Please destroy the board. It is more dangerous than you can imagine. This is no joke. A little over the top? Maybe, but true. If it gets my point across...

THIRTY-ONE

Real Event

The Mexican Monolith

In 1984 I met my brother, sister-in-law, and my parents in Cancun, Mexico for a vacation with the family. We had a wonderful and exciting time. We decided to travel west to see the Yucatan Peninsula which is where Chichen-Itza is in the middle of the jungle. Chichen-Itza is a Mayan city that contains the Pyramid of the Sun. An imposing structure that juts out of the jungle into the sky. It was insane being driven there by my older brother. He has a big lead foot and it was especially heavy that day. We got there in one piece but encountered an accident on a two-lane road with the jungle on each side growing right up to the edge of the asphalt. When we toured Chichen-Itza I experienced odd flashes of insight about the place. The guides were wonderful. The guides were adamant that their ancestors came from an island east of Mexico that in the past had sunk into the Atlantic. I remember the "vibe" was a mix between mystery and death but as you probably realize by now, I am a bit sensitive to certain phenomenon. Nothing clear in my mind but a feeling of familiarity to me as if I knew this place. We then drove across beautiful open farmland where Blue Agave was grown just to make Tequila. We arrived in Merida, the capitol of the Mexican state of Yucatan. We spent the night in a lovely hotel, toured the city the next morning, and headed north to Progresso. It reminded me of a Mexican version of Panama City in Florida. On the way there we noticed a sign pointing the way to a new archaeological dig site that was open to the public. The site was a Mayan ruin called Dzibilchaltun. When we arrived, we drove up to a parking area and got out to stretch our legs. When we were there in 1984 and it was just recently open to the public, not a developed site with an information building with water fountains and bathrooms. When we were there, we were free to walk about with no restrictions. It is open now but no one is allowed in certain areas. The moment we started to walk into the site what seemed like a million yellow butterflies surrounded us with the most wonderful greeting I have ever had. There were so many the sky turned yellow for a moment. I could feel the breath of their wings on my face.

They are known as Mariposa, a native to Mexico. They landed on us by the hundreds and stayed with us for a few minutes then disappeared as fast as they arrived, it was a beautiful, incredible moment.

I noticed that the site was large, many city-blocks long. We walked down an avenue that was a least a hundred yards wide with crumbled buildings being painfully restored to their former glory. At the far end of the plaza what looked like a dwelling that might have been equivalent to a City Hall? But what drew my attention was in the middle of the plaza was a large flat pyramid platform with a large monolithic slab of stone that was at least 10 feet high on the center of the platform. Like in the movie *2001:*

A Space Odyssey where the apes gather around to touch the monolith, I was compelled to touch this monolith. When I reached out to touch the stone I was engulfed in a living vision, including the sounds of people, the smells, and the heat of a typical, hot dry day here. I looked around and just knew I was there in real time. There were people with me on the platform with their wrists and ankles bound. This was a slave market along with many other items being traded and sold. When I touched the stone all my senses came to life. I was simply present in a time long past. A time slip perhaps? I could see the people as they were. I was bombarded by the smells of food, sweat, urine, feces, and animals. I could hear a language vaguely familiar, the sounds of busy people and even music and dancing. To say it was incredible is an understatement. This was a marketplace much like Chichen-Itza was a multipurpose city for games, worship, human sacrifice, astronomy, and the seat of the rulers with a pyramid of the Sun.

I later told my friend Carol, what I had experienced and her reply was "this is what a clairvoyant experiences in a vision." Clairvoyant means "clear vision" in French. Clear vision indeed! It was the only time I have experienced such an event. I wish I could do it again, it was incredible. Carol also taught me to see suras. Hers is golden and sometimes white.

THIRTY-SIX

Real Event

Conspiracy Theories, Heaven's Gate Cult, and the Atlantean Power Crystal

At various times during 1988 I started attending a local UFO group and I met three people that would have a great influence on my perceptions of reality and on my life. Howard would drive down from Clinton, a small town in the Ozarks. We talked for many hours and he opened my eyes to possible conspiracies behind the politics in America and the world. Before I met him, I was innocent of the politics of the world. History was not what I had been taught in school it seemed. At first, I had a hard time believing him. Most, but not all the information was true but what was, has proven over the years since to be much bigger than even he knew. He presented the information in a calm and honest manner. As time went on, I began to understand what he was saying. I no longer remember the details of those conversations, but the core of them centered around a cabal of very powerful, influential elites who were directing the paths of human societies and the fates of nations to bring the world population under a new world order. The cabal is now revealing itself by their arrogance and the overt thrust of their agenda. Over the years as things have evolved and things have been revealed, it has been shown to me in downloads, that these elites want the return of an Oligarchy, ruling over and controlling the willing masses using technology. A Technoligarchy utilizing A.I., manipulation, and surveillance. China has already implemented this into their society. We are all witness to the crumbling of the most powerful nations in the world. Possibly a part of the final plan to create a level playing field amongst all nations so no nation can rise to defeat the final plan, the final solution to reduce the human population on this planet to a much smaller number. It is now happening. Many nations are losing population faster than they can reproduce. A smaller population is easier to control. The Covid-19 pandemic was most likely the first wave of their plan. Many millions have died, mostly the elderly and infirmed. The population of China has been severely reduced. My friend, Teddy, who I mentioned earlier, was one of those with co-morbidity.

Then there was Candy. Candy is no longer with us. She lost the battle with Metastatic Breast Cancer in 1996, a few short months after a confrontation with the Heaven's Gate group so famous for committing mass suicide to hitch a ride on an alleged spaceship in the tail of the Hale Bopp comet. The Heaven's Gate group visited the Eureka Springs UFO Conference seemingly to recruit new members just days before their departure from this reality. They had surrounded Candy when she demanded they leave because they were causing a disturbance.

Candy had written a few books on various subjects relating to aliens and UFOs. Some were about a race of aliens that infiltrated our secret societies and governments to bring about massive changes in population using propaganda, mind control, and surveillance. Her theories dovetailed neatly with Howard's information the same way detectives take testimonies from different witnesses and piece together a crime scenario.

Then there was Carol. Carol was unique. We could say she was very sensitive to her surroundings on many levels when it came to spiritual matters. Her information dovetailed into the information Howard and

Candy had provided as well, much was on a spiritual level. A few months after we met, which I still do not have a clue or memory about how it happened, soon after she invited me to her home for a talk and lunch. After we talked about various things of interest, we sat down to watch a video on Marcel Vogel, an IBM team inventor of the LCD screens and the Hard Drive used in computers. The documentary video was about his later years when he worked with Quartz crystals. Carol sat behind me to my left as I sat on another chair in front. Between us was a side table and a swag lamp hanging over the table. We had watched for about 30 minutes while talking about our adventures with crystals when, for no discernable reason, the swag lamp incandescent bulb just exploded throwing shards of glass all over us. I do not mean the filament popped; I mean the bulb exploded. I am seventy years on and I have never seen that happen except in movies, (those bulbs are special effects rigged to explode). We tried to figure out what just happened and realized that the swag lamp was in a straight line in between us. You tell me? Some would say that it just happened, no big deal. Except that it could have happened at any time but it occurred the exact time we were together. For all the weeks and years that it could have exploded it was the right time. My guess is there was some powerful connection between us and there still is. We are still great friends to this day.

Interestingly, she is one of these people that cannot wear wrist watches or use electronic devices. They simple do not work around her. I built a computer for her and had to connect a grounding wire to the mouse and computer frame to keep it from dying. Electronic equipment would just die.

She had already knocked one out a few months before. Her being sensitive to spiritual information somehow increases the electrical energy in her body. It is a tradeoff, I guess. We talked for a long time, and it came out that we had known each other for a very, very long time over many lifetimes. Carol explained that she recalled being a priestess in the Temple of Poseidon in the city of Atlantis. She said that I had been a scientist working on very important technology including the energy source of the Realm. Edgar Cayce, a famous psychic in the 1920s spoke of the Great Crystal of Atlantis being able to transmit energy to power the great city, ships at sea and even flying craft. I find it poignant that Nicola Tesla was almost finished constructing a power station called Wardencliffe that would transmit energy wirelessly to power many homes for miles around. It was a test facility, but funding was removed by Tesla's Financier, J.P. Morgan because Tesla had not included a way to charge people for their electrical usage. My guess is that metering was to be included later but Morgan still dropped his financial support.

It should have worked but it just devastated Tesla and he fell into decline never to recover. I ask you, is it not possible that Tesla could have been a citizen scientist of Atlantis? A friend or co-worker perhaps? If you are not familiar with Nicola Tesla read his autobiography. He is one of the greatest inventors ever, almost lost to obscurity. He was THE most influential contributor to our modern electrically based society.

I find it very interesting that many individuals who have studied ancient Egypt have theorized that the great pyramid was an electrical generator and the obelisks were receivers of that power. I have much to say on this topic in Part Two.

Sorry, I digress, Carol claimed that I had been seduced to entertain dark things while I worked on the Great Crystal projects that could cause great damage and she was afraid for my life and soul. According to Edgar Cayce, the Great Crystal that powered Atlantis became unstable and exploded with a force of many hydrogen bombs. Apparently, the force of the explosion was enough to lay waste to an entire city. Carol compassionately claimed that I had something to do with the great crystal's destruction. I felt on one hand incredulous, but on the other hand, it seemed familiar and possible and when she told me this, for I had felt a great guilt out of nowhere, sadness and remorse and I wept. A great weight was lifted off my shoulders that I must have carried for a very long time. As I look back in time what I was working on was not located in the capitol city of Atlantis per se. Where I was must have been a colony of the empire of Atlantis. There are many possible locations that this destruction could have happened. It may have been a colony on the coast of Greenland. Who is to say the Atlanteans did not have colonies? One wisely does not play with powerful forces in a populated area.

According to the writings of Plato the capital city Atlantis sunk beneath the waves in one day and night and was lost to history, never to be available to modern man. The surviving Atlanteans spread out across the world helping to rebuild what remained of humanity. Eight of the wisest were known as the "Followers of Horus" who I believe were the great teachers of modern civilization. I believe the Azores is the location of the capitol city of Atlantean Empire. The Azores is exactly where Plato claimed it was beyond the Pillars of Hercules or the Strait of Gibraltar. The Azores sunk under the waves as the sea rose around it by around four hundred feet during an Extinction Level Event or ELE, we now call the Younger Dryas event. Is Atlantis real? I have memories of living there but cannot say for certain, however, I am convinced that technological based societies existed before the Younger Dryas. Much more on that subject in Part Two.

FORTY-TWO

Real Event

A light in the hallway, Probes and Night terrors

In 1995 I was involved as a video contractor at the Eureka Springs UFO conference. I worked it for several years and met and befriended many wonderful people.

To say the attendees were strange is a bit harsh. For the most part, they were passionate about finding the truths of the paranormal. They are just like you, wanting to understand and get a straight story. Most were there seeking knowledge and confirmation of their own experiences that had flamed the fires of their curiosity ranging up to and including damaging trauma. The odd ones are usually the ones that see things first. Many of the strange events around the world happening now, we spoke about many times in the 1980s and 90s. All were there seeking kinship and the sharing of their experiences with like-minded souls just wanting the truth without skepticism from others about what is happening even to this day. I learned many things and it opened my mind further, to very interesting, strange, and downright challenging concepts. Over the years since that wonderful time in my life I learned a secret. Do you want to know what it is? Good! You probably have heard the phrase the "The universe only gives you what you can handle." That is true up to a point. However, the universe abhors the status quo, it may give you what you can handle but it knows you better than you know yourself and if it feels it is time for you to grow to your greatest potential it will challenge and push you until you learn what you are here to learn. As farfetched as this may sound, the universe is conscious, it is alive, it is IAM, and very much aware of literally everything happening everywhere in real time through quantum entanglement. It is the child creation of God after all.

There was an episode of a TV show in the sixties that had a starship crew investigating a beautiful planet. Odd things began to happen to everyone in the landing party. It turned out that the planet was a machine that read their minds and created whatever their minds thought, conscious or unconscious. Some were delighted and some were killed. They had to be very careful what they thought about. This was an entertaining analogy for life. More on this later. You may feel that sometimes the universe or that life is against you, take comfort in the fact that the Universe is like a machine that was constructed for several reasons by our creator for you to live a life to learn who you really are. So, the greater the lessons the harder they are to learn. Anything worth having or experiencing is worth the effort. Like you, I have been challenged to learn. Some experiences that I learned in the remaining part of Part One of this document are some of the examples.

Some of these lessons occurred in my home. For example, one night I had just spoken with a friend on the phone I had met at the local UFO group conference and lived in my city, offered me several books and tapes on UFO lore. I thanked him but declined his offer and I asked him why he was getting rid of them. He claimed he was having some strange events going on in his house that were upsetting him and his family and that he was moving to another state out west, I think it was Washington. I told him I was glad he was my friend and I wished him and his family good luck in their new adventure. The call finished up about 10 p.m. which is the usual time to for my wife and I go to bed. Before our boys came along, we would sleep with the bedroom door open to the hallway. It was not more than a few minutes after the call; I had just laid down and I had my eyes open and a blinding flash of white light lit up the hallway. And no, the light did not explode! It was not on at that time. My wife experienced it too. Remember, I had just spoken with my friend about strange occurrences in his house and now it was happening in my house. This was just the beginning.

It terrorized me and my wife. Was it hysteria or was something trying to tell me something? It was events like these that contributed to our divorce a few years later. It turns out that divorce is quite common in the UFO field.

Many simply cannot handle it, and I can understand why.

I have kept my bedroom door closed at night ever since then. For the next 12 months or so nightly events continued and increased in intensity and continue to this day. If I remember correctly a few nights later in the same hallway I remember seeing two orbs that were an orangey-red color floating just on the inside of my now closed bedroom door. They lasted about 20 seconds and faded away. About a month later I woke up lying on my back on the left side of the bed with my left arm exposed. Floating just to the left of my arm about the same height was a cubed shaped object about 3 inches long on each side, it was dark and metallic with some designs and what I discerned were some kind of sensors bristling out from every side. I watched it in terror and yet curiosity as it floated inches from my left arm for about 30 seconds and it just vanished. Obviously, it took some time for me to go back to sleep. A couple of months went by without any events until I went to take a shower and get off to work, I noticed in the vanity mirror a VERY large bruise on my right thigh midway down to my knee. The closest shape would be a baseball bat impression. To my surprise it was just a little sore. Besides having a bruise, I have no idea how I got it in my sleep, it faded away by the next day. Every normal bruise I have had over the years would take many days or weeks to clear up.

The next occurrence was again in my bed. Again, I woke up on my back, my arm at my side but this time there was another "probe" hovering inches above my left arm. It was shaped like a green neon corkscrew tube. It was about 12 inches long and about 3 inches in diameter and glowed dimly. It spun slowly, taking its time doing whatever it was doing then in a blink it was gone.

On at least three occasions, maybe more, many more, I had terrifying visitations by what are now called Greys. A closet is on my left side of the bed and I remember seeing one crawl out of the closet and stood above me to my left. Another came out of the bathroom door facing the foot of the bed and what looked like a naked female grey with stringy black hair. I woke the next morning with a very sore penis and urinary infection. My wife never knew what had happened. I also had a long black hair wrapped around the base of my penis. This also happened to a very good friend around the same time. He had one black and one red. We contacted a UFO researcher and found that testing the hair was very expensive. The last one I recall dropped out of the ceiling right above the bed and straddled me, getting inches from my face. With my wife asleep next to me and the covers holding me down there was little I could do. It seemed to be probing into my thoughts. I got the impression it was interested in my fear which I definitely had. It stayed there just looking for a few seconds and I passed out. What really blew my mind was that there is a working ceiling fan in the area it came through what I could only guess was some kind of portal. It seems they can go wherever they please with complete disregard for the laws of physical matter with almost an arrogance in their mastery over the forces of nature. I understand your incredulity. It is just as strange to me as it is to you.

I was so stressed out at that point I became tired of being scared and became very angry and aggressive.

One night I spoke aloud and I told them if they came back again, if I could, I would tear one of them to pieces. I projected my anger and aggression as images of the terrible things I would do to them. I have not seen or been aware of their presence since that time. That is not to say they have not been back; I just have not been aware of them. A few weeks later I remember being strapped to a table. It was oddly dream-like, however some researchers believe that some abduction experiences could be astral events. To my left about three feet away was a structure that may have been a wall that was jet black with a grid of what looked like red LEDs dimly lit. I was lying on a table with the panel to my left. That is all I remember.

Things slowed down for a while but continued to happen.

FORTY-FOUR

Dream Vision

A Sad Reunion

In October of 1986 I got married to a wonderful woman, Janet. In 1995 and 96 we had 2 sons. Both healthy and happy. Things settled down for a while. My father left this world in the fall of 1996 just before my second son was born. He had a massive heart attack with the same issues my grandfather had that I mentioned earlier. Do you remember the dream I had after he died? The one about sitting and talking on the warm sunny day in the mountains? Well, it happened with my father as well. This dream however was not so pleasant. You see, I loved my father but we had issues just like many millions of fathers and sons have. He was definitely "a glass half empty" kind of guy. He had a hard time accepting and living a life with positive, productive thoughts. His experiences on Okinawa during the war in the Pacific must have affected him in a very negative way. When I was young, I remember him often coming home upset and frustrated with his customers and he would often take it out on his sons. It created a situation of distrust with us and him. He almost always saw the darker side of things. It was difficult for me to learn to be positive about life because of the environment growing up around him. However, a few years after his first heart attack, he mellowed out and was much more loving and forgiving. A few months after he passed on, I had a meeting dream/astral event with him. Also, the last time I saw him. I remember it well and I also remember never telling my mom about it. It would be simply too upsetting for her. These dream goodbyes are very common. Most people do not talk about it because they just see them as dreams. However, these dreams are very real and significant.

I remember in the dream being in a small, dimly lit room. He was lying on a cot like what is used in an Army encampment. He had his right wrist placed on his forehead. He looked scared so I asked him what was wrong. He said he was scared he had cancer again. You see, he had prostate cancer about 10 years before and it was traumatic for him. The surgical techniques were not very good at the time and he was in a lot of pain. I think this trauma spilled over into the dream experience we were sharing. When he was still alive about a week before he died, he told me that he had been bleeding. In the dream I told him gently that he did not have cancer but that he had passed from a heart attack. Sadly, he did not believe me. But then again, he never believed me or so I thought. I told him he would be all right and not to worry about it anymore. At that point, I woke up feeling very sad for him. I prayed that he would get the help he needed. Fear and stress, exists on the other side as well. I am totally convinced he was literally scared to death contributing to his heart attack.

Note: Please remember this, what you worry and stress over in this life you carry on to the next life only amplified. This is why it is important to control your thoughts and emotions here in this world. Thoughts and emotions are instantaneous with full impact. When you have a dream that is easily and quickly forgotten, that IS a dream. When you have a dream that you not only remember very well with many details but sometimes it can be a moving, even a profound experience. This is NOT a dream; this is an astral experience. Astral travel can and often feels like a dream but is more coherent, more memorable.

A meeting dream is when you have a conversation with or just see a loved one or good friend. There are things said, such as goodbyes for the last time. They have stayed around in the astral level waiting to say things unsaid in life then they move on to even higher realms but you will see them again and you might say your goodbyes to loved ones you have left behind some day. If you have these dreams treat them with care and realize they are not just dreams. They can be a wonderful, loving occasion.

FORTY-SIX

Real Event

A Star Gate Confirmation

In 1999 I was working as a copier technician. I had attained a level of competence and confidence in the eyes of my supervisor to take a newbie out for training. He was bright and quick. Of course, we talked about his past work experience. During our conversation he revealed he had electronics training in the US Air Force. We had much in common. We then turned to talk about his military experiences. He was an electrical technician which prepared him for working on copiers. Somehow the conversation went into strange territory.

For a few years I had worked as a videographer at the Eureka Springs UFO conference. One of the speakers was a respected gentleman from England. You could tell by his demeanor that he was a cut above the rest. He was calm and subdued and very knowledgeable. I worked with him on his presentation and got to know him and admire his work. He had just completed a book called *Above Top Secret*. His name is Timothy Good. I procured a signed copy of his book for my library at home. When I got to read it, I was spellbound. I remember in his talk he mentioned a source formally in the United States Air Force (USAF) who had a troubling experience during his tour of duty. His story that I remember, went like this. He had been given an assignment to a special mission that was apparently top secret. He claimed he was escorted onto a helicopter that flew him from the U.S. mainland to an oil drilling platform in the Gulf of Mexico. At least it looked like an oil drilling rig, it even had roughnecks working a drilling system. He was dropped off and escorted to a door that led into the bowels of the rig. This was not just an ordinary oil drilling rig.

It was disguised as such but was controlled by the military. He was uneasy about the situation. His escorts accompanied him to what looked like a common freight elevator. He and his escorts walked in and the doors closed. He waited for the elevator to move, it did not. There was a hum and he felt nauseated and disoriented. After a few seconds the door opened and he stepped into a hallway that ended in a large room. There was bright sunlight streaming through windows and desert outside. He was very confused and again disoriented and I am sure he was apprehensive. This could not be! He had just been in the Gulf of Mexico just moments ago. An officer dismissed his escorts, saluted him, and greeted him. "Welcome to Pine Gap, Australia sir." Are you as confused as I was? He had been in the Gulf of Mexico one minute got in a box and instantly was in the middle of Australia. Incredulous? As Carl Sagan once said "extraordinary claims require extraordinary proof." I concur.

The young man I was training that day to work on copiers made an extraordinary claim. As I said he claimed he had been in the USAF. He claimed he had a very high clearance. Being an electronics tech, you cannot help but see things going on around you. He never said which base he worked or I just forgot. The extraordinary thing is what he said next. He was told to report to an officer on his base to be escorted. They met and proceeded to what looked like a common freight elevator. He stepped in with his escort, the door closed and the elevator did not move, it hummed. He felt nauseated, dizzy, and disoriented. Only a moment passed and the doors opened. He passed down a hallway and he said, "I felt kind of light on my feet." He walked into a large brightly lit room that had many people at computer screens. His eyes had a hard time adjusting to the light because it was an orange red glow from outside a large window. He was looking at desert with a red sky. Then it happened! He said, "I was not on Earth!" I asked him where was he? "I was on Mars!" I did not say a thing! I got a distinct chill down my spine. Neither Tim nor the Newbie have ever met, nor do they know each other. Their stories were far too close to be just a coincidence. Over the years I have heard unconfirmed stories about other similar stories. You decide??????

FORTY-SEVEN

Real Event

Nasal Surgery and a Revelation

In 1990 I finally had enough of the issues with my sinuses. Living in a humid state pretty much assures one is going to have sinus issues. I have had sinus headaches since I was 20.

I made an appointment with a very seasoned, old-school ear, nose, and throat doctor. He was a very odd fellow but luckily, he was an excellent doctor. He had no idea of what personal space was. Most people speak a few feet away from each other but he would have many conversations with me an inch away from my face. I am so glad he did not have halitosis. He gave me a very thorough examination. "HHMMM, that's interesting" he said. He then asked me his relevant questions. One came up that stood WAY out from the others. He asked me if I had nasal surgery any time before that day. I was shocked. I said "no, why?" He exclaimed that I had surgery done sometime before and that he was surprised how it was such an expert surgery. A cold chill went up my spine. I was more surprised than he was. I never told him what this diagnosis may have really meant. He never said what kind of nasal surgery had been done because he had never seen such precise work before. Now, I was concerned, and shocked again.

What I do know is that is: 1) I have had headaches even to this day on the left side exactly where he claimed the surgery had been performed. 2) During this time of my life many thousands of people all over the world were claiming they had been taken by extraterrestrials (ETs), now known as non-human intelligences (NHI) and had implants inserted into their bodies at various locations and many people have had implants removed by qualified surgeons even these days. 3) I had many spontaneous nose bleeds at night when I was very young. A sizable number of people claim to have implants in their brains and believed to be inserted through their sinuses and some have shown up on x-ray and CAT scans.

Note Implants: If you are one of many who are not familiar with alien implants, I will do my best to explain. Implants are claimed by many alleged abductees and doctors alike to be devices implanted without their knowledge or consent in different locations in the body. Some are advanced organic constructions; some are electronic and some are completely unknown to our current science. Some are even combinations of all the above. I have seen or heard of them being inserted into necks, behind the ear, in the hand between the thumb and palm area. Some are placed in the lower calf or thigh areas and as in my possible case, in the sinus cavity just beneath the brain. All implanted without any damage to the skin and no scarring. I would not be surprised if there is an implant in my head, the evidence points to that possibility.

I am sure there is much speculation what these devices are doing both passively and/or actively. It is a safe guess that they some are tracking devices such as we use to track animals in the wild. Some could be active for such uses as feeding information to the implanted person or direct communication. Some could be a form of mind control but that is still pure speculation. We will probably never know the true nature of these devices.

FIFTY

Real Event

The Elemental

At the most stressful time in my life, I experienced something to this day that intrigues and bothers me at the same time. You see, I was heading into a divorce. It is stressful for everyone who goes through it. Your relationship is falling apart, how are you going to survive financially and of course, and the children always suffer the most. All this and more were coming to a head.

The experience is so controversial, so out there that I am still hesitant to reveal it. Let it be known that I am taking a substantial risk here. I had already experienced so many crazy things in my life but this tops them all. I sincerely ask that you read this with an open mind, do not make a judgment one way or the other and just absorb it at this time. This entire subject is so emotionally charged, so controversial it begs for special treatment. I have already paid a heavy price for revealing this to people around me who I thought I could trust. I ask you to let your mindset be open, seeing that there is so little we know about these rare and seeming impossibilities. Just as we have come to understand over the past decades, we have discovered that the universe is much, much larger than we could ever guess. As you are experiencing now, we are beginning to see the world is stranger than we could ever believe and, it is getting stranger every day. Sometimes what we call reality can be stranger than fiction.

I hope I have opened your minds to the potential for this to even be thought of as real. I know it was. Anyone with a very rational mind would be certain that I am insane, and at the very least suffer flights of fantasy. I assure you both are untrue. My understanding of what my teachers have explained to me is that there are many layers of different realities existing in the same space as ours even at this very moment. Physicists now agree this is fact. Not only dimensional layers but that every known and unknown possibility of moments in time from the distant past to the remote future all exist in this moment enfolded in the space around and within us. We are just not aware of them because our consciousness is limited now to three-dimensional space-time, the moment we are in now.

Our five primary senses have evolved over millions of years to allow us to function efficiently in only three dimensions. I realize this is a strange concept but this is proven by science and mathematics.

Have you ever wondered what existed in the space thousands of years ago that your home exists on now or what it will be like when your home is gone, what replaces it in the future? Or am I the only one who thinks these things? We exist in only a blink of an eye in geological time.

Remember, God or the universe only gives you what you can handle and just a little bit more just to push you along willingly or not to make you learn and grow.

Let us go down the rabbit hole together. Here goes nothing!

It was a normal routine weekday, nothing special, just got home from work. I walked into my bedroom and started taking my shirt off when I caught something moving. I froze. My bedroom door is parallel to the bathroom door with the foot of the bed right between the two. When you come into the bedroom and turn left and you can see a four-foot gap between the foot of the bed and the doorway into the bathroom. Moving to my left between the bed and the bathroom door was something, I still to this day find it utterly fantastic. Imagine if you will, a bubble approximately 7 inches in diameter, transparent with a silvery, pink, lavender hue. It moved just over the carpet from behind the bed toward the bathroom doorway to my left. Inside was a little creature that was beautiful, not just to the eyes but something else. I felt wonder and a great privilege just to have seen it. It turned its head toward me and smiled, yes, smiled as it went through the bathroom door. I was so stunned that it took me a few seconds to react. I stepped a few steps forward, enough to see into the bathroom. Leaned over to peer in the bathroom door. It was gone. Did I just see what I think I saw?

[1] Stockton, S.A. (2003) photograph reproduction.

This photo above is an exact reproduction in the exact location in my bedroom.[6] This is what I saw. The color and size are to scale. The only difference is the missing elemental. The frame of the bathroom door is to the left side.

 Are you old enough to have used an AM/FM radio in your vehicle? If not, I will introduce you to it. Before CD's, MP3, MP4 and SIRIUS radio there was AM/FM radio. Most of you probably listen to AM/FM radio even now. When you are traveling long distances and you lock on a great station, great tunes, then the signal starts to fade out and you just cannot leave that great station, that great tune. Then occasionally before that fading station is completely gone another station tries to override that eat station. Then finally the great station fades away and a Spanish station comes in. It may not have happened to you but it has

----

happened to me many times. You see, there is a circuit in your FM receiver called a Discriminator. Its job is to distinguish station strength of signal and lock onto it. When the signal is reduced to its minimum level it gets harder to distinguish the separate signals so they can sometimes overlap each other. You may be asking what does this have to do with a little creature in lavender, pink silver bubble. OK, think of it this way for a moment. Imagine, if you will, that what we call "Reality" exists as a frequency range just like the stations on the radio. Imagine again that there are other "Stations" or frequencies we cannot see or experience.

The FM dial has a range from 88 to 104 Megahertz. That is a very large range of frequencies. When you are locked into this station, "reality" frequency it is very hard to experience" hearing" any other station's "reality" other than what station you are locked into. So, we know there are other station's "realities" out there, but we cannot experience them. Just like the discriminator circuit failing its job, sometimes there is a disturbance in the reality circuit that allows two or more frequencies realities to crossover and bleed into each other. This will start to happen more frequently in the years to come. I am convinced what happened when I saw the lavender bubble creature was a crossover event either in my awareness or a breakdown in the fabric of space-time, a merging of two parallel "reality" frequencies. A glitch perhaps? My mind was open at that moment to receiving other frequencies. My mind, at that moment was not occupied with other thoughts.

If you are saying to yourself at this point, "this man is wacked out"? You can believe what you want, it will not change the reality of the universe. I have been checked twice by professionals. One told me that I had Adult Attention Deficit Disorder. That is all. Understand that I am going out on a limb here so that others will be brave and reveal their truth to the world. I assure you, there are many millions like you and me. Maybe, after reading this document you will understand you are not alone. Be brave in your truth.

FIFTY-FIVE

An Egyptian Merchant Dream Vision

One of the many Dream Visions of possible previous lives, this one was vivid, more than most. I remember sitting on a blanket on a dusty street on a hot, sunny day. I wore a dark, loose robe and had many trinkets at my feet. I must have been a merchant.

I sat on a corner of two streets. It was a prime location to sell my trinkets. To my left was a broad street that I could see many people going about their business. To my right was a side street that was a market space. Coming from my left, looking around the corner was a group of black men pulling ropes that were attached to a large stone block. They were sweating, I could see it glistening in the bright sun. I remember feeling sorry for them. I could smell the many foods, dust, sweat, and the smoke of the cooking fires. I turned my head back to the front when I heard someone ask me something about what I was selling. I was consumed by the heat and dry air. I heard a scream back to my left, around the corner. As I turned my head again to the left, I saw several people pointing away from me down the street. People started screaming then they started running toward me.

The entire street erupted in screaming and terror, abandoning everything. As they ran past me and I saw a gap open to see what they were running from. I was stunned, terrified. Up in the sky about a hundred feet in the air were three golden discs in a chevron formation shining in the sunlight. They were beautifully terrifying. They approached my direction slowly as if they wanted everyone to be in awe. I knew these were the gods; they had to be. That is the last thing I remember. The dream ended there.

Dream Visions? A dream that is not a dream could be a download of any sort of information from any source. It is sent or unlocked for the reason to enlighten, to inform, to warn or to inspire. Understand that dreams are another reality, another level of existence, but just as valid as this reality. The Aboriginals of Australia consider their dream world to be more real than our waking world.

This vision was sent to remind me of an important part of my existence, that I must have lived a life in Egypt at the time of the gods made themselves known to the people maybe for the first time. I have a passion about the history of Egypt. This dream vision links reincarnation and the ancient gods of Egypt and Khemet, two of my most fascinating interests. I feel from the vision that the day in my vision was the first day of the god's arrival in Egypt. Can you imagine the terror and excitement that would have caused? After all these years I can still remember the vision well.

FIFTY-SIX

Real Events

A Potato Chip, Remote Viewing, and the Human Operating System

While working the video production in Eureka Springs UFO Conference in 2009, I had a hilarious experience. I have since realized that I should not take this all too seriously. My crew and I took a lunch break just down the street at a great barbeque place. We had a great meal and friendly conversation. Almost as we were finishing, I had one last potato chip. I was about to devour it when something on it grabbed my attention. Right in the middle of the chip was a hole. I looked harder at it. I laughed out loud at the irony. Here I was at a UFO conference and the potato chip had a hole, the shape of a flat-topped flying saucer. How crazy and wonderful this world is to give me such a gift at the perfect time. We were all amazed and amused. I just had to show this to the conventioneers. Since we were on the video crew, why not.

I put the chip in front of the camera and as I was doing that, the crew master got on the microphone and announced, with tongue in cheek, that we had found a UFO just down the street. "Does anyone want to see it?" YES, everyone replied. When the image came up on the projector screen the rather sizable crowd erupted in laughter. What a fun memory.

The first event of that year makes me giggle every time I remember it. It was one of many synchronistic events in my life. These fun events have convinced me that the universe has a crazy sense of humor. If the universe is a computer simulation the programmers either were lazy, crazy, or just too tired to work out the bugs in their universe simulation program. Glitches in the matrix? What are the chances that someone would attend a UFO conference and find a potato chip with a hole in the middle shaped just like a flying saucer, oh, excuse me, an Unidentified Anomalous Phenomena (UAP). During my time working the video production at the Eureka Springs UFO conference, I purchased a device called Questor. It is a device that synchronizes the right and left hemispheres of the brain creating a neural pathway connecting each half to create a more coherent brain connections utilizing complete brain capacity. Utilizing the Questor often, the brain may make new neural pathways to connect each hemisphere for greater capacity much as meditation rewires the cortex. I still use it today.

The device has a controller containing programs and controls for the different functions like volume, speed, etc. The device had headphones to produce binaural beats and the last component is a pair of sunglasses with two LEDs mounted on the inside of each lens. All you can see is the flashes of light from the LEDs. These again are controlled by the main control unit by producing various patterns of flashing of light combined with the binaural sound pulses synchronize the right and left hemispheres of the brain. It is much like a strobe light going off in your face with your eyes closed. By selecting different programs, one gets different experiences. External inputs allow music to be mixed in. The flashing patterns produced by the LEDs created various, beautiful tunnels of light as well as a host of colors which was entirely unexpected. When the program ends one can perceive random dots of lights. These random dots, that look like noise on a TV screen, could very well be overstimulated neuron traffic that begin to recede or fade away. I would say that because everyone's brains are individual, the effects may be different.

I have had two significant experiences so far revealing some very interesting results with Questor.

With the first experience I chose a program to help me relax and focus my attention. I added external music. Nothing happened at first. As my brain became synchronized or "rhythm entrained," in my mind's eye I remember descending from space to a planet. I immediately recognized the features of Mars. I did not slow down like one would descending in a ship. I dove into the surface and came to a stop inside a vast cylindrical structure. It was dimly lit like someone would leave an office at night with just a few lights on. Standing at the bottom floor and looking up it had to be at least a thousand feet to the top floor. I estimate it was about three hundred feet in diameter. It had an open area all the way up with circular railings on each floor.

Each floor extended out from the main shaft with corridors radiating outward. On each floor, which all looked the same, in from the railing was a wide-open walkway. I noticed in the dim light were large, transparent cylinders approximately eight feet high, hundreds on each floor, radiating outward from the core of the building all the way to the top floor. What I saw in each cylinder chilled me to the bone, so much so that I retreated away, back to Earth, back to my comfortable sofa. The cylinders contained human beings in some type of suspension. Alive or dead I do not know. Who does this storage facility belong to? Is it a human facility or Martian? Were we Martians before we lived on earth? Why are humans being stored here?

It has been the only time I have experienced Remote Viewing. Remove viewing is the ability to obtain information in an extrasensory way, such as sensing or seeing what is in a location without physically being in that location. It feels much like astral projection without the astral body.

The second experience was totally mystifying, I have tried to repeat what I experienced this time again with limited success. Again, in my mind's eye I was floating in a vast space with a huge, wide screen. It was curved and covered my vision almost to the edges of my mind's eye with just a little of the space around me being visible. On this vast screen was a grid of squares. Inside each of the thousands of squares were rapidly flashing letters and/or symbols. The speed at which they were flashing made it hard to discern what language they were. However, I believe they may be Hebrew or possibly Sanskrit. I have repeated this experiment many times. It is entirely possible that this language is completely unknown yet I discerned it is of advanced technology or divine in nature. It is entirely possible the language may even be non-human. They may not even be a language as we know it. By using the Questor, I may have discovered what I would call a Human Operating System much like an Operating System of a conventional computer, which I viewed on a massive computer screen in my mind's eye. A human operating system that governs the mind, body interactions.

A system that makes us well, us! Is a human operating system so farfetched? Our DNA is an operating system based on bio-chemical processes that produce and maintain our bodies. Our cellular structures are literally nano machines processing chemicals, hormones, peptides, and proteins commanded by our DNA using sub programs called RNA. Could a holographic code create our souls based on a replica of the God source code? The Bible claims in the book of Genesis that we are made in the image of God. Could that be literal? Holograms are 2D in form, projected as 3D images. With proper stimulus we may be able to view this hologram within our own minds.

Currently there are experiments ongoing utilizing a scanning laser and Dimethyltryptamine (DMT). Smoking DMT and looking into the scanning laser's image, many claim they have observed a 3D world beyond the surface reflection of the laser including changing code within the 3D space/image. This is very similar to a 3D hologram. This is admittedly far-fetched but what if it is real? This has far-reaching potential if true. This could be an entirely new science studying the underlying structure of the universe.

This Operating System, however, is much more complex and ancient than any program today or even in the near future of A.I. My theory is that it is a self-activating, self-programming, adaptive software program written by intelligences unknown. Any thoughts beyond this level on my part would be complete conjecture.

If you want to investigate for yourselves, I would recommend purchasing a left-right brain synchronizer online. I am certain the units available today are far more sophisticated than the Questor I used.

FIFTY-NINE

Dream Vision

The Gift

In 2012, that famous and stressful, scary year for all, I had a most vivid dream vision experience, the kind you remember forever. It was what is now known as a lucid dream, that is the dreamer is aware that they are dreaming. It also may have been an astral experience, all the same, I was totally aware of everything. I was floating in total darkness. It was peaceful. What I perceived as up, I saw high above me, a white, flagging, translucent object floating down like a falling leaf. It was descending, floating toward me and the closer it came the more rigid it became.

The white object decelerated and positioned itself as if it would descend over me as if it was to be my coffin. It stopped and hovered just above me as if waiting for something. I sensed a benevolent intelligence from it. You see, it was not physical in any sense of the word. I intuited that it was a fourth or even fifth dimensional conscious machine. Imagine if you will, two large clear plastic diamond shapes fused into each other at one end of each. These diamond shapes were large enough to house my body and configured like a coffin with my head at a point of one diamond and my feet at the opposite end of the other diamond shape. It had, close to each opposite ends, large cylindrical holes like they had been drilled through each diamond. The interior was almost clear but had a smoky quality to it.

I heard in my head a female voice asking me if I would accept this gift. I truly felt no trickery or malice toward me. So, I accepted the gift. As I confirmed the gift, the machine started shrinking and descending to enclose me. I thought for a second that it would crush me inside but it did something odd. It continued to shrink, passing the boundary of my skin. I could feel it inside of me with no pain at all. It felt wonderful, and I was delighted.

There was a brief flash of energy in my nervous system, much like the accent into astral travel and I perceived that it had locked in. It stopped shrinking at about 2 inches long and positioned itself into my heart chakra, my sternum area. When it was completed, I was told information about it, but the message was scrambled so I would not remember at that time. I can only assume that this gift was for some future use, and it may be some sort of protection as with a magical symbol. That is just a guess. Hopefully I will find out what it is at the proper time. Remember, each form has a individual sound pattern and every sound has a form pattern.

The above image I created from my memories of the object.[7] This precious gift was not just given to me but

---

[7] Stockton, S.A. (2012). Image of object.

maybe to all of us. I have researched this with no luck to find anything remotely similar or any explanation of what it is or symbolizes. I now believe it is to be what we, as a species make of it. A symbol of hope and a new beginning perhaps. It could be a magical symbol for our protection. Let us make it something wonderful, beautiful and a hope of an awakening within us all.

SIXTY

Dream Vision

A China syndrome

On the 31st of March 2013 I had a terrible nightmare about a nuclear reactor plant here in my state. I saw in my dream the control room with people scrambling to find out what was going on. I dreamed it was in a China syndrome situation. This is when the core of the reactor goes into criticality creating an uncontrolled meltdown. Also, the power turbines "tripped" which means, because they are spinning so fast and have such rotational, kinetic force, they must be shut down slowly; a controlled shutdown. I woke in terror. It was so real. Turns out it was real but luckily, not as critical as the vision dream portrayed. Early in the morning hours of April 1, 2013, engineers were in the process of moving a 525-ton turbine core when the crane's cable snapped sending the turbine core smashing to the concrete floor. The impact was so strong the remaining turbines did trip and shut the power down coming from the plant. The impact registered on a Richter scale as a minor earthquake in that area.

Subsequently, a young man was crushed under the machine and several others were injured. In the dream I recall the feelings of sheer terror of the men involved and had visions of people running around like ants. Maybe I was feeling the men's terror.

I have often had dreams that have come true, unfortunately they were so long ago I cannot recall them except this one. It was not entirely the way I saw it happening, but the result was the power plant shutting down. I do not have a definitive answer, but I will give it a try. Two things can converge to create a situation like this. One, we live in a universe that is constantly sending out waves of energy of various types and frequencies. Those waves propagate in all directions spatially and temporally. When events happen involving extreme emotions such as terror, it can send forth very powerful energy waves that may be felt by people all through space and time and sensitive people can pick up these waves easier than others that are less sensitive.

A case in point, Prof. Roger Nelson headed a project known as the Global Consciousness Project that consisted of computers placed all over the globe. These computers, known as EGGs, or ElectroGaiaGrams would do nothing but process a string output of random numbers and send that data to a collection server at Princeton University that would create a visual output showing a pattern of order midst the chaos. When a significant world event was about to occur such as 9/11/2001 the randomness of the output would become inexplicably less random and therefore more ordered.

An output of order occurred 4 hours before that fateful morning. This would hint at a phenomenon that even machines can react to these energy waves moving through space and time.

Understand that thoughts are energy, emotions are energy and the two together are an immensely powerful combination. When two or more waves of energy such as light they create a hologram of manifestation

within the universal hologram. When I saw in the news about this project. I emailed Roger Nelson and we communicated for a while about the process, yes, it is real.

SIXTY-ONE

Gaia Vision

Real event

As much as I could, I would visit a favorite site on the western end of the Petite Jean Plateau. It overlooks a vast stretch of the Ouachita Mountains and forests. I have always loved this place. It is a place of peace and reflection.

On a hot September day, I sat down on a large rock to enjoy the warm sun and eat my lunch, wind and the vultures gliding past me watching me with their keen eyes. I felt a strong urge to relax my breathing and open myself up to whatever came my way mentally.

From deep within I felt a profound sadness, anger, and loneliness. At first, I did not know what it was. I felt the spirit of Gaia speaking to me, not in words but through Gaia, Greek mythology's Earth goddess: the powerful, spirit consciousness of the earth. Yes, as crazy as this may sound the earth is a living being. It is female. We have a very limited idea of what life is. People used to call it Mother Nature. Shyly I asked how she felt and asked her for understanding. The instant I asked that question out of the vast sky before me came a wasp. It slammed into my face stinging me under my right eye with just enough pain to get my attention but not enough to cause harm. I felt a great sadness. This was a profound moment for me. I am certain that wasp was the answer to my question. She is angry, sad, and unloved by mankind. We are using her up! Stealing her life away. She is the earth, fire, water, and air element sources of our physical being, she birthed our race from the very stuff of her being. She is the mother of all beings on this planet, something we sadly do not realize and take for granted, always taking, never giving back. Native Americans knew her as "the Great Spirit." In a film from the late 1990's humans were compared to viruses. It is a stinging declaration but sadly it is true. I remember from childhood reading the Bible where it says that man shall have dominion over the earth. This is an extremely arrogant and narrow-minded declaration. For one, we could and never will have dominion over nature. We were supposed to be stewards of this planet not her rapists. We have tried the dominion path and look where it has gotten us? We are not even stewards of this world. This is the very attitude that has gotten us in this terribly destructive way of thinking and living. Because generations have considered nature to be hostile to us, we have warred against the earth since. I ask you; would you treat your mother this way? I feel for her even now as I write this document. We are not sensitive enough to even be aware of her existence yet. We must become aware and soon. We must ask her forgiveness and maybe, just maybe we can live in harmony again with her and have not only her forgiveness but her blessings again upon us. If we do not, we may very well be destroyed much like viruses invading our bodies. We have been destroyed before in the ancient past and we may yet be again.

These thoughts may be considered by some as trite yet they are significant to our survival. We live in an artificial world designed purposefully to perpetually produce worker consumer drones in a vicious circle of money flow and endless wars. A system to perpetuate a lower vibrational frequency of endless want, always looking to the future that never arrives. Always moving, never still to reflect. Never living in the present. A system that is completely unsustainable and is eventually doomed to fail. And when it does, what will we do? We have punched the ticket for a train ride to extinction. Yes, it is a depressing scenario. Why are more people than ever consuming anti-anxiety and anti-depressants? Because we are all asking the same silent question, "is this all there is to life on this planet"? We all live in a world of control and fear. We are so fearful of making the wrong decisions, we have become stagnated. We live in invisible prisons without even knowing of their existence and of course the invisible keys are in our hands. There seems to be no clear path to redemption. We are quickly reaching the end of an era of a technologically induced nightmare fueled by extremely sophisticated social media and consumerism creating canyons in place of bridges. Tribalism and fear have reached divisive and paranoid proportions so much that amid the most advanced communications network the world has ever seen, we are more isolated, polarized, and alone than ever before.

We have reached the age of pure Individualism. There is only one way out and I will elaborate in Part Two.

SIXTY-TWO

Real Event

Three Knocks

In 2015 I was alone in my house, it was around 3 a.m. and I was having a hard time getting to sleep. Something was just off that morning. My house is clad in wood panels that resemble slatted wood. I was awakened when I heard three powerful knocks on my bedroom wall right behind my headboard. The headboard moved with the impacts. BAM... BAM, BAM. Then again BAM...BAM, BAM. While my heart was racing, I listened carefully for minutes afterwards. No more knocks thank God. My heart was pounding. I heard nothing, nothing at all outside like bushes rustling, footsteps, not a sound other than the normal night sounds. Nothing. I have learned over the years through documentaries about hauntings and conversations with people that know more about the subject than me that any demonic presence will commit acts of evil mockery of holy events such as the crucifixion of Jesus at 3 a.m., the opposite of 3 p.m. I am not sure what pounded on my house, but sure it was not human.

SIXTY-THREE

Real Event

Falling Things

In late September of 2016 I took a solo trip to New Mexico, Utah, and Arizona. It was primarily to photograph the west and specifically a Slot Canyon known as Antelope Canyon in northern Arizona. It is a photographer's dream come true. It is a very narrow, small canyon formed from erosion over millions of years of red sandstone. It has beautiful organic forms that flow with how the water flowed over the years shaping them. I had prepared to sleep in the desert with all the provisions I could think of, only the problem was that September in the Arizona is their Monsoon season. It rained every night. I had planned to make my way into Hopi territory to spend a week what they would let me experience of their culture but it is was not to be. The more the rain fell at night the more my funds dried up.

So, I cut the trip short by going through northwestern New Mexico. It was raining of course, and I was exhausted by the time I got to Farmington, a very nice town in the middle of nowhere. I decided to stay at the first motel that came my way. The first one I found was a nineteen sixties design but comfortable on a rainy night. I slept well. The next morning, I took a shower. I had my razor, liquid soap, and shampoo. I placed them on top of a ceramic soap holder, the type that was popular in the fifties and sixties. It was designed with a shower handle on top and on the bottom section it would hold a soap bar, very solid. I lathered up the shampoo and started washing my hair, blind of course from the shampoo in my eyes when I heard the razor drop on the shower ceramic floor. I felt around and found it and put it back up on the soap holder. It fell again after a few seconds. I picked it up again, put it back on top of the soap dish. As I rinsed my hair and got the water out of my eyes the shampoo dropped on the floor. I laughed; this was some funny stuff. As soon as I put the shampoo bottle back the liquid soap bottle fell off. What the heck was going on? I made sure all three items were back on top and decided to watch them. As I watched, the razor moved a little. It moved again enough to fall again, but I caught it midway. Now I thought is there a secret camera on me, is someone getting a good laugh at my expense? Was there a camera watching me? I checked to see if the soap dish was normal, it was. I continued to watch as the shampoo moved across the soap dish handle. It seemed as if it was being pushed a little at a time until it would fall. In the process of bending over, picking up the shampoo the soap whizzed past my head. This was too funny. As soon as I stood up straight the razor fell again. I quickly finished and grabbed my shower items and climbed out of the shower laughing. I dried off, got my clothes on, and got out of there.

When I checked out, I asked the clerk if he knew if anyone had died in my room in the past. He gave me a quizzical look and smiled. No one that he knew of, but that motel had been there a long time before he came along. Motels and hotels are replete with ghost stories all over the world. I felt no earthquakes or heard rumbling trucks hitting a pothole. I am pretty sure a spirit was having a big laugh about me.

We all have abilities to attract different types of people into our lives, some good and some bad. Attracting ghosts? This event had me scratching my previously very wet head. I do not really think I attracted a ghost to my hotel room; I think this ghost was living there in that room I just happened to sleep in. This ghost may not even know it was dead and was confined to the hotel room with me. Sometimes I wonder if these ghosts see us as ghosts and are confident that they are the living ones and we are the ghosts. It was a very amusing occasion in that old hotel in Farmington, New Mexico.

SIXTY-FIVE

Real Event

A Red Ring

Two days after my sixty fifth birthday I woke and looked in the mirror after taking my morning shower when I spotted something. On the right side of my stomach area of skin, right over my liver was a perfect red circle mark about 1 inch in diameter. It looked like I was jabbed by with the end of a pipe.

It was bright red but not bleeding and it never hurt. It had completely healed by the time I got home from work. I have absolutely no idea how it got there, and I did not hurt myself in any way the previous day or night. This is my actual photo:[8]

---

[8] Stockton, S.A. (2018). Photo.

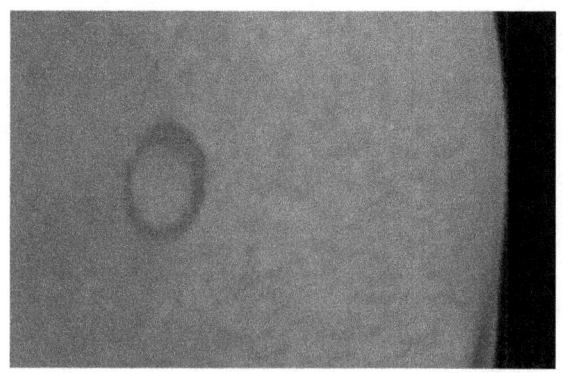

I have only one theory about what this circle is. My days of being visited in the night may not be over. Could it be a mark left by some device possibly medical in function?

Maybe some intervention? I can only guess what it was. However, please do not assume I just accept these events as only supernatural. Yes, I have an open mind but it is definitely not a sieve. I am getting older after all. In Part Two I will explain how I use both sides of my brain, the logical and the contextual side. Did you think I was going to say illogical? I jokingly think that most left brain dominate thinkers believe right brain dominant people are illogical. I am a lefty and therefore a right brain person and remember we lefties live in our right mind.

SIXTY-SIX

Real Event

Two Red Rings and Claws

On January 6, 2020, I again woke, took my morning shower, and looked in the mirror to find the same kind of marks. This time there were multiple marks that were more complicated. This time there were two red circles the same diameter, less defined but both had red dots in the exact middle. Adjacent to these circle marks are what look like three or possibly four fingernail scratch marks. I have again, no idea how they got there. Again, they were gone by the end of the day.

I certainly do not heal that fast and I do not know anyone else who does either. One could suggest that I hurt myself on something and did not realize it at the time. This is a plausible suggestion. But the problem is that I was a couch potato that day and night watching television. I encountered nothing that could have done this. As wild and crazy as this is, I may have another possible explanation. I have seen marks like this on people claiming to have been abducted to do medical intervention, procedures to humans they are interested in. And besides that, remember when I was eight? I had medical procedures done then as well. Remember the nasal surgery that I never had but the doctor said I did?

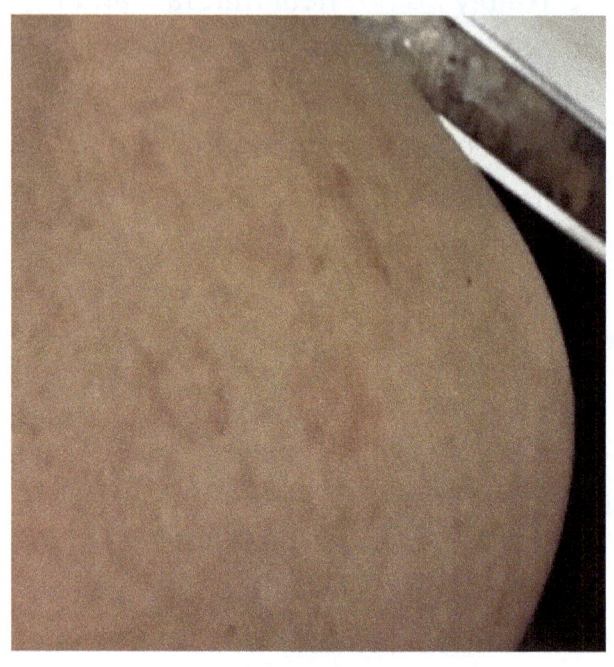

This time two circles and fingernail scratches.[9] This did concern me. The two circles with red dots in the middle look like medical instruments for certain. But the claw marks were even more concerning. It smacks of being man handled or even WTF handled. I

---

[9] Stockton, S.A. (2020). Photo.

took this photo the morning of discovery.

You are probably thinking I did this to myself and rightfully so, but I assure you I had nothing to do with it except being the recipient. I am as puzzled as you are.

The above photos were taken by me. The first was taken on 10.25.2018 and the second was taken on 1.06.2020. The first one is not enhanced; the second one is color and sharpness enhanced to show more detail. My stomach is not that large; I pushed it out to take the photo! I really would like to have had a smart phone when all these other sightings and odd phenomenon were occurring in my past.

SIXTY-NINE

A Shot in the Dark

Recently I found yet another mark on my body when I woke up. I am convinced now that something or someone is monitoring my health and possibly taking corrective measures, I hope to keep me healthy. This latest mark looks like an injection site on my front left thigh that was a little rough. Note the bruising. For some strange reason it did not heal for many months.

The only reason I can imagine for all this attention to my health is to keep me healthy enough to write this document??[10]

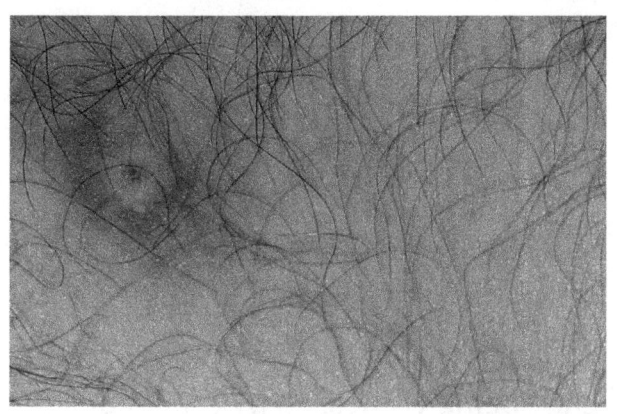

Stockton, Stephen (2023). Photo.

There have been other experiences in my past, and some are happening even now. I have had seven other UFO sightings that were just that, sightings. Some looked like zigzagging star-like objects that were obviously under some kind of control either internally or a drone of some kind. Some were white rod-shaped objects that looked too thin and small to be manned and I have seen silver spheres that would pass over me well inside the atmosphere but no sound at all.

And one I photographed with an early digital camera that was witnessed by three other people with me acknowledging their sighting with me but it did not show up on the camera image for some curious reason. The craft being witnessed by others but not picked up by my camera suggests a phenomenon experienced by consciousness not necessarily recorded by machines such as a camera. I find that very interesting. This phenomenon has been reported over the years by other experiencers.

As you read this your mind may be saying "this is a bunch of nonsense." I understand completely. I was much like you in the beginning of my journey. Understand, if or when you witness an UFO or UAP, I promise you, you will never be the same! It will shake you to the core of your world view. It will free your mind; it will awaken something deep within your being. If you find it hard to believe any of this document, believe this, for it is a truth so profound it is the truth you have been looking and waiting for your entire life.

If any of you have already experienced something this profound you know I am speaking the truth. I know many who have been changed forever for the better. I sincerely hope it happens with you.

Chances are if you have not had an extraordinary experience yet, you will in the next few years. Great things are coming. A new world awaits! Expect the unexpected!

Addendum: As I finish this document I remembered two additional events in my youth.

When I was twenty in 1973, I had two experiences I had forgotten. Since I have retrieved those memories, I can now share them with you. The first involved a common occurrence in the proximity to an anti-gravity craft. The energy field they produce depletes electrical energy from everything around them.

The night was cool with clear skies. I was traveling south on Interstate 430 as I was crossing over Col. Glen rd. My car was running fine. As I came down an incline my engine just died. Lights and displays died as well. Since I had Rack and Pinon steering, (unpowered), I could easily control the car off the pavement onto the inner median into the grass. I got out to "take a look" at the engine and found no problem, it was just dead. At first, in my concentration of my immediate circumstances, I failed to notice something very unnerving. I was not alone. Within a few hundred yards around me there were at least five other automobiles also dead, some still on the highway. I then realized there were no sounds, no lights, it was dead quiet. No crickets, no cars, nothing. We were all out of our cars looking at each other in bewilderment. After about five minutes our autos started up. I drove away, scratching my head and I am sure the others were doing the same.

The second one was just as unnerving. At this time, I had two friends named Jerry and Jeff. Jeff lived in Foxcroft, an addition to the south of where I lived in Overlook Park at the time. Jerry had the only car between us. It was a dark blue 1966 Mercury Cougar. Very nice car. One morning Jerry and I were heading to Jeff's house. We had just turned right off Indian Trail rd. onto Tallyho Lane. What we both saw to our utter amazement was a dark blue 1966 Cougar passing us in the opposite direction, onto Indian Trail. There were two young men in that car just like us. As we passed each other, all four of us were just staring at each other. I know you will think this is impossible but for that brief, insane moment there were two Jerrys and two Stephens. In recent years many stories of time slips have been published. I have no clue how or why this could happen but it did.

CONCLUSION

PART ONE

When someone brings up the subject of their dreams most people find it boring. I hope you found mine interesting and thoughtful. I would truly hate to bore you or give you no hope for the future. I have great optimism for the future overall. I am assured there is a plan in action. A plan to right the wrongs of the elites.

All my memories are correct and true in every detail that I remember. Yes, memories can be flawed. However, when you have these types of experiences you will remember them very, very well. They are seared into your mind forever. They are a part of me now. They make up a large portion of what I am and what has shaped me. The reason they have significance here is that they relate to the discussions yet to be revealed. I wanted to give you a heads up with them to set the stage, structure, and flavor of the rest of this document in Part Two. Sprinkled here and there will be additional life lessons learned and I want so much to share the awe and wonder of the things learned and there is so much more to come. I consider myself to be "normal," whatever that is, a person with all the bumps in the road of life just like everyone else in this crazy thing called life. I have been told all my life that I am strange, weird and "out there." I used to take these opinions personally and it hurt me deeply, but no longer. Maybe it was for a reason. I was being programed by friends and family members in the way I should act but as life continued, I learned to transmute these insults and rejections into a positive affirmation that I just might be doing it right this time around. You see, when someone criticizes you such, it reflects the fears of rejection by others that they project on to you as a deflection from their own doubts and fears about themselves. As you get older and hopefully wiser you find that everyone is unsure about life, about their place in the world, insecure in their relationships, even in their own existence.

I hope to show you that your life is a precious gift to be honored, not abused and by honoring it you honor the creator of all and when you honor the creator it responds in kind many times greater. And when you truly honor others, you honor God and they will, most of the time, honor you. This is the core of the Golden Rule: Do unto others as you would have them do unto you.

In these times, humans all over the planet are finding it hard to keep their sanity for the world is getting stranger, crazier, more hysterical, more insane every single day and it is accelerating. Some have called it "The Quickening," likening it to a birth of a baby, a new way of living. One of the most of true truths I have ever come across is that "misery loves company" so the miserable will not feel alone. By themselves they make as many people around them as miserable as possible.

Currently the world is in this mode and it seems everyone is as miserable as possible. Sadly, we share our misery more than our joys. When we project misery into the world that is what we receive in turn. We often get what we ask for but only if it serves to teach us something. That is no way to live and/or be happy, yet mostly we do it unconsciously, because of our self-destructive nature. If we think of negative things we get a negative reaction. Thoughts are energy. Like the butterfly effect, small things affect the whole within a closed system and this planet is a closed system. What we project into the world, what we think is real becomes real and then is reflected to us and that again changes our thoughts and attitudes, mostly reinforcing what we already believe.

It is my sincere hope that we can learn together how to peacefully change things for the better. The alternative is nothing less than a disaster. Sincerely listening openly to others thoughts and their opinions shared with you without judgement is a wonderful start.

Part One of this book being a true documentation of my life's events, I must tell you I had many other events that just do not warrant mentioning here because the memories are fragmented and disjointed, more like dream states. I have also experienced

Close Encounters of the First, Third and Fourth Kind. So, I wanted to only include the events I remember and to give you the reader the most accurate information possible.

Peace and joy to you!

Look for Part Two coming soon!

If you think you have gone deep into the rabbit hole just wait till you see what comes next!

EMAIL:
TLOD.book@Yahoo.mail